Volume 3

Awakening
the workplace

Achieving Connection, Fulfillment and Success at Work

*To Bell.
You are my
inspiration and
my friend forever.
love
Ruth*

Editors: Adele Alfano and Kathy Glover Scott ■

Published by
Experts Who Speak Books
www.expertswhospeakbooks.com

ISBN 978-0-9780283-4-3
©2008 Kathy Glover Scott and Adele Alfano

Editors: Kathy Glover Scott and Adele Alfano
Book design and production: Creative Bound International Inc.
www.creativebound.com

Library and Archives Canada Cataloguing in Publication

Awakening the workplace : achieving connection, fullfillment and success

at work / editors: Adele Alfano and Kathy Glover Scott.

ISBN-10: 0-9780283-0-9 (v. 1 : pbk.).—ISBN-13: 978-0-9780283-2-9 (v. 2 : pbk.).—

ISBN-13: 978-0-9780283-4-3 (v. 3 : pbk.)

  1. Quality of work life. 2. Success. I. Alfano, Adele, 1959-

II. Scott, Kathy Glover, 1958-

HD6955.A94 2006   650.1   C2006-901559-7

Printed in Canada

Contents

Introduction

The spark for *Awakening the Workplace* first came to light during our initial planning session for Experts Who Speak Books in 2002. Even at the dawn of our series, as editors we were passionate about communicating the new knowl-

edge and tools needed to address the changes and daily challenges in an ever-evolving workplace. *Awakening the Workplace, Volumes 1* and *2* are now international bestsellers, also published in Asia. *Awakening the Workplace, Volume 3* is the eleventh book in our acclaimed Experts Who Speak book series.

With all of the Experts Who Speak books, our goal is to provide you with tips, tools, motivation and essential information. In *Awakening the Workplace, Volume 3*, you'll find the collective wisdom, experience and knowledge of 16 top speakers, trainers, facilitators, coaches and consultants from across North America who specialize in workplace issues and innovation. Where else can you find the proven expertise and essential wisdom of 16 top trainers, coaches and consultants in one book? Each have taken the absolute essence of their work and teaching and condensed it into chapter form. And the information in each chapter is written with a focus on providing you with the new tools, skills and systems you need to excel, all in a format that is easy to read and reference.

What makes *Awakening the Workplace* volumes unique is how they speak to the reader in a solution-focused way, regardless of their role in any size of business or organization. How we execute our workday has rapidly changed and many of the old rules for how we should work together have been challenged—or thrown out altogether. Yet, there are threads of knowledge and expertise that all people who work require. *Awakening the Workplace* reflects the need for this multi-faceted information.

Experts Who Speak Books is one of the most successful book publishing companies in the world specializing in producing books for professional speakers, trainers, facilitators, coaches and consultants. We create co-authored books that showcase the dynamic, creative and successful people who have chosen these professions. We do it through supporting the writing process and taking care of all the specialized work of design, printing, publishing and distribution. And, we do it from a win-win value base, where cost sharing, cross promotion and mutual support are the keys to our success. You are invited to visit our websites:

www.AwakeningtheWorkplace.com
www.ExpertsWhoSpeakBooks.com
www.SalesGurusSpeakOut.com
www.ExpertWomenSpeakOut.com
www.LeadershipGurusSpeakOut.com

Watch for our next books, *Leadership Gurus Speak Out, Volume 2*, as well as *Awakening the Workplace, Volume 4*. Subjects for upcoming books in the series include the Internet, communications and marketing. Let us know if you are in these professions and would like to contribute.

All in all, you are holding in your hands a goldmine of information and expertise, geared to make your work life easier. Our wish is that success flows to you. The choice is yours—to remain where you are or move forward. Not a hard decision to make!

Kathy Glover Scott and Adele Alfano
Editors and Publishers, Experts Who Speak Books

Michel Neray

www.EssentialMessage.com

Everything Starts With a Conversation

Picture this. You're out having a coffee with a friend. After a few minutes, an acquaintance of your friend happens to walk in. He comes over to your table, says "Hi" to your friend, and you get introduced. Then he sits down to chat with both of you. After you finish talking about the weather or how busy it is in the coffee shop, the inevitable question comes up: "So, what do you do?" You've got 60 seconds. Go!

Typically, there are three ways that people answer this question—whether the question is asked while standing in the coffee line, at a networking event or from across the boardroom table in an actual sales presentation.

If the best you can muster is sales manager or sales rep (or consultant, or lawyer, or accountant, or whatever is written on your business card), you are using the most boring of the various answers you can offer—and you've just blown an opportunity to find your next client or get a referral. Reading your job title and company name off your business card is about as engaging as reading a list of ingredients off the side of a soup can. It communicates that you are either embarrassed about your job or not particularly interested in talking about it.

The second way that people typically answer that question is with a clever phrase that they've developed for exactly this situation. Or perhaps they've memorized their positioning statement. You know what a positioning statement is, right? Here's a typical formula: "We help (target group) achieve (obvious benefit) by (activity) so that they can (ultimate outcome)."

If you're one of those people, don't give yourself a pat on the back just ye You're using the most annoying of all the different ways you can answer that question. After all, your positioning statement or any clever phrase that you might have come up with is formula-based, rehearsed, contrived, and—face it—boring, just like those dreaded elevator pitches and infomercials.

Yes, every business should have a positioning statement, and everyone in the company should memorize and internalize it. But please don't speak it! Your positioning statement may be clever and clear, but it's not conversational or friendly, nor is it engaging. You might as well have a loud, flashing neon sign above your head that's screaming, "sales pitch, sales pitch, sales pitch!" And all the while, the only thing that the person in front of you can think of is, "How quickly can I get out of here?"

So, let's talk about the third way that people typically answer the question, "What do you do?" If you've ever gone to a networking event—the kind where everybody sitting at the lunch or networking table gets a turn to describe their business—chances are you've heard it dozens of times. You know when one person is going on and on about what they do, and everyone around the networking table politely tunes out or stares at the person's business card. Then, when they're finished, nobody has a clue (and couldn't care less about) what that person actually does for a living.

I call it the "drunken, barroom brawl" technique because it looks like a bad fight scene in an old cowboy movie. The person at the networking table throws out a series of disconnected statements, like a drunk in the saloon who keeps swinging punches in the hope that one of them will connect. And, if that's how you answer the question "what do you do?" then you, like many people, have again just blown an opportunity to find your next client or get a referral.

A Symptom of a Bigger Marketing and Sales Problem

Consultants, advisors, entrepreneurs, emerging companies and, indeed, most salespeople are between a rock and a hard place when it comes to how they describe their business or introduce themselves at a coffee shop or a networking event. To start with, there's no way you can sum up everything you do in a neat little phrase. And to make things worse, once people know what you do, they lump you in with a half million other people who, on the face of it anyway, appear to do the same thing!

So does that mean you have to be in "sales mode" all the time? Heavens no—especially if you believe that being in sales mode means being pushy and manipulative. The truth is if you can't articulate in a compelling manner who you are, what you're especially good at, and why anyone would want to do business with you, then chances are, the same vague and uninspiring "non-sales" messages permeate your entire business—on your website, in your brochures, in your sales letters and emails, and in your advertising. And it's often a symptom of a deeper, more fundamental sales and marketing problem.

To prove it to yourself, take a look at your website, as well as the websites of some of your competitors. Or flip through some of your recent proposals and sales letters. Do you see anything that engages your prospects and speaks directly to *their* interests? If you're like most people in business, the answer is probably "no."

Your Essential Message is absolutely the most basic part of all your sales and marketing, and yet most businesses skip over it. Without your Essential Message, it doesn't matter how many salespeople you hire or networking meetings you go to, how many ads you run or brochures you send out, or how many people view your website—all your sales and marketing require more effort, response rates are less than optimal, and it's harder for you and your salespeople to establish credibility.

With your Essential Message, on the other hand, you get people's attention more easily. You inspire the people you speak to about your business. You know what truly differentiates your business from competitors. You are absolutely confident about the value you offer. And most importantly, you communicate it naturally and conversationally—there's no hard sell.

If you can see the link between those things and increased sales, read on. That's what this chapter is about.

Throw Away the Rule Book

No doubt you've heard very specific instructions on the "correct" way to create a positioning line, or the "correct" way to write an elevator speech or infomercial. And of course, everyone knows that you have to focus on high-level benefits and avoid negative statements, right? One of the biggest reasons people have so much trouble with positioning and articulating a compelling message about their business is that they are working from somebody else's rule book. Let's just look at one of those so-called "rules"—the one about focusing on or leading with high-level benefits.

To understand why benefits aren't the be-all and the end-all of marketing, pick a benefit—any benefit. For example, if the product or service you sell helps your client's bottom line, you might think that "make more money" would be an extremely attractive benefit.

Brian Smith helps his clients make more money. So does Barbara Henderson. In fact, Fred Baker and Olivia Chow also help their clients make more money. However, here's what each of those people does: Brian is a financial planner. Barbara is a meat broker. Fred and Olivia are sales reps for a major software company.

In other words, most people and businesses, regardless of the product or service they actually offer, can claim the same ultimate outcome.

Telling your prospects that you'll help them—insert any high-level benefit, for example, "make more money" or "increase productivity"—is usually as impactful, credible and differentiating as a politician saying he or she supports world peace.

Part of the problem lies in the language itself. We all *think* we understand what features, advantages and benefits are, and as a result, we fail to see that those terms are, for the most part, interchangeable.

In other words, what could be a feature for one person is a benefit for another. And how *you* might define the benefit of your product or service may not have any relevance to your best prospects.

So how do you figure out what to say in print, on the Web and verbally? I suggest you begin by eliminating the words "feature" and "benefit" from your vocabulary. You'll find it far more useful to think in terms of *impact statements* and *persuasion drivers*.

Impact Statements

You know you hit on an impact statement when, in the course of a conversation, the person in front of you raises his or her eyebrows, leans forward with particular intent, or expresses genuine interest. An impact statement, therefore, can best be defined as anything you say (related to your sales conversation) that results in a significant, positive reaction from the other person.

Persuasion Drivers

Ask the person you're speaking to what it was about that (impact statement) that they found so interesting. When you have your answer, you have your persuasion driver.

A persuasion driver is the reason your impact statement triggers an impact with the other person. The reason may be extremely personal or it may relate to a universal experience. Whatever it is, however, simply having a conversation about it helps you uncover even better, more motivating impact statements and persuasion drivers. And it shifts the focus of the conversation from "all about me" to "all about you" (which you probably know from personal experience is always more engaging for the other person).

Write Your Own Rule Book

If there's one thing I hope to illustrate from the example above, it's that features and benefits are theoretical concepts in someone else's rule book, while impact statements and persuasion drivers are based on what really works for you. Once you throw away the rule book, you can begin to write your own. Here are three things you can do to get started:

1. Attend a lot of networking events

If you think that networking events are just for trading business cards, you've just found another reason to throw away the rule book. The most valuable thing you can take away from a networking event is not a bunch of business cards, but rather all the research you could be accumulating on your Essential Message.

> **Think of a networking event as a giant focus group. Attending it helps you figure out what resonates most with people about your business and the true core value of what you offer.**

Michel Neray

As you work the room, try emphasizing different aspects of your business or what you are selling. Ask a lot of questions about the kind of service the person you are speaking to would like to receive. And most importantly, pay special attention to the reactions you get.

If you truly listen, you might be surprised by what people find most interesting and appealing about your business. Write these things down! These are your impact statements. Over time, you'll develop a heightened awareness about what your best prospects are looking for, and you'll experiment with different ways to incorporate these things into your conversation.

2. Ask your best clients and customers

Clients aren't usually shy about telling you why they like doing business with you and what attracted them to you in the first place. If you're reluctant to ask them, get over it! Tell your client that you need their help to understand your business better. Be clear that the purpose of getting together isn't about asking for new business or referrals, although new business and referrals often result from these kinds of meetings.

Be prepared to probe. When they tell you they like the quality of your work, ask them what they mean by "quality." And when they tell you they get the feeling that you really care about their success, ask them what it is exactly that makes them feel this way.

Remember, what may seem commonplace or obvious to you may be extremely important to your clients. You'll never know unless you ask.

3. Lighten up and let your passion out

A big part of determining your Essential Message is allowing more of you to show up in everything you do. That simply won't happen if you're too serious or overly concerned with appearing "professional."

To illustrate, let me ask you this: Have you ever hired a nanny? How about a dog walker or an auto mechanic? Probably the first thing you noticed is how much (or how little) the person enjoyed what he or she was doing, right? Instinctively, we all want to do business with people who love what they do, because we intuitively make the link between what they are passionate about and what they are truly great at. But if you listen to most people in business, including salespeople, they talk as if what they do is the most boring thing in the world.

Listen to yourself next time you're in a new business meeting. How inspired would you be if you had to listen to yourself for an hour? So why is handing over your child, pet or car any different from your client giving you business? The real question you might ask yourself is, "What makes me afraid to let my passion show?"

There are at least a few reasons you may be keeping the passion you have for your business under wraps:

- You might think that you shouldn't make it look easy or enjoyable, because if you do, it may not look valuable enough;
- You might be afraid to "invest" yourself in a new relationship in case it doesn't work out or you get rejected;
- You might think that showing any excitement will make you look childish, silly or, heaven forbid, unprofessional.

Remember that no amount of technique can mask a lack of passion—and nothing fires up a conversation quicker than a spark of passion. Lighten up and let your passion out. Your customers, clients and prospects will thank you for it.

Five Ways to Start a Conversation Around Your Essential Message

Instead of trying to come up with a clever phrase that will "magically" engage the other person in a conversation, ask yourself this: "What can I say that will make the other person want to engage me in a conversation?"

Unfortunately, there's no such thing as a magical phrase or headline that will make the other person want to buy your product or services—it just doesn't exist.

What does exist, however, is an approach that will elicit interest from the other person so that he or she will want to engage you in conversation around your Essential Message. And if you've done your homework by talking to dozens, maybe hundreds, of people at networking events, in social situations and in client meetings—you may have already identified the impact statements and persuasion drivers that work the best.

Now it's time to put on your copywriter's hat and get to work. You're going to write out the conversational equivalent of the headlines you might write if you were preparing a magazine advertisement for your product or services. The following are five of my favorite conversation starters:

1. the provocative question;
2. paint a picture;
3. the level-setting statement;
4. address the stereotype head-on;
5. the straight goods.

Let's take a look at each one separately and see how you might adapt it for you.

The Provocative Question

The provocative question is one of the best ways to help you define your Essential Message in "customer-centric" terms. Chances are, you've seen this technique hundreds of times on websites, flyers and direct mail. It's Copy-writing for Direct Marketers 101, and it works just as powerfully in verbal conversations. This technique is called provocative questions, not because it's intended to be argumentative, but rather because it *provokes thought*.

For conversations, such as those at networking events, the best way to come up with a provocative question is to ask yourself the following:

What question can I ask, such that the response from the other person allows me to say, "That's what I do…"?

The best provocative question pinpoints a problem or a symptom of a problem that the other person has. However, don't get trapped into thinking that the problem has to be a big, generic problem that the category as a whole solves. It can be a small but nagging problem, or even one that people have when they deal with your competitors.

If the answer that gets conjured up in the other person's mind is, "Yup, that's an issue for me," you've got a good provocative question.

If the answer that gets conjured up in the reader's mind is, "Wow, I don't know, but I sure need to find out," you've got a *great* provocative question!

Many people have a hard time coming up with provocative questions, because ironically, the most compelling ones are so simple and obvious. Here's an example. When someone asks me what I do, I often answer back with a provocative question like this:

"Well, let me ask you a question. When you go to a networking event or when you have to introduce yourself in public, how confident are you with the way you describe your business?"

In the vast majority of the situations, the person acknowledges that he or she doesn't feel confident with the way they describe their business. In that moment, I have engaged the other person's interest by presenting what I do in a way that's personally meaningful to him or her. Then, what generally ensues is a conversation about the sales and marketing challenges they have and how I can help.

That's my Essential Message.

You might be wondering what I do if I get a different response. What if the response is something like, "No problem, I am totally confident with the way I describe my business at networking events and in public situations!"

If this happens, I congratulate them on being so clear about how they present their core message. In the conversation that follows, the other person might come to the conclusion that core messaging is so important to all their sales and marketing activities that it's worth exploring further, or they might give me a referral of a business that would find my services helpful. Alternatively, I might simply move on to another provocative question.

It's all good.

Now you might be thinking, "I see how this can work in one-on-one situations, but what about when I am addressing a large group?" The truth is that provocative questions work in any situation. You can use them in presentations and seminars, in small group networking events and in formal sales presentations, as well as when meeting informally over coffee.

If you can get over the "rule" that you have to always introduce yourself with your name (which no one ever remembers anyway), then you'll find that the provocative question will work for you, too.

Michel Neray

Paint a Picture

This is a variation of the provocative question. It involves using the same impact statements or persuasion drivers that you used for your provocative question, but here you use them to paint verbal picture to illustrate the challenge or problem the other person might be facing.

Start with, "You know when..." or "You know how..." in such a way that you can describe a challenge that your best prospects have. When you see the head nodding in agreement, you can continue with, "Well, what I do is..." Using the same example as before, here's how "paint a picture" would play out:

"You know how some people go to networking events and when it comes time for them to describe their business, they flounder about and they're not really clear about who they are, what they do and the true value they offer..."

You can see how it serves the same purpose as the provocative question, but "paint a picture" allows you to start a conversation in a less direct, more gentle way.

The Level-Setting Statement

If you're a financial advisor, consultant, or in any other crowded profession where your prospects are very familiar with—perhaps even jaded about—the kind of work you do, pay close attention.

The level-setting statement is a universal statement that gets the other person nodding in agreement and then—WHAMMO!—your point of difference hits them like a ton of bricks!

Here's why it's such a powerful technique. You can only be different in comparison to something else. That's what the level-setting statement does—it establishes what that something else is. The following are three examples that came out of a workshop I presented:

"There are five specific areas of expertise that are absolutely critical in major event planning, and it's extremely unlikely that any one event planner would be an expert in all of them. Because I've been in the business for 15 years—on both the corporate and the vendor sides—I've developed a detailed planning process around

each and every one. That's what enables me to track and manage the myriad of details to guarantee a successful event."

"There are a lot of good insurance agents that can do a fine job of serving your personal needs. It's also not hard to find a good insurance person to help you with your business needs. But if you're a partner in a professional services firm, or an owner-manager of a business with employees, you also have to look at your key personnel and group benefits. And what's even more important is making sure that all your insurance—for your business, your family and your employees—is integrated, so that you don't have too much in one area, and not enough in another. That's what I do."

"Marketers typically try to help you develop your point of difference around the classic professional variables such as niche, problem solved or results, but that ignores what is potentially the most compelling differentiator: the personality and passion of the individual. When you think about it, what's more unique than the individual? That's why in all our marketing exercises there's an added element of self-exploration that adds tremendous clarity into why you do what you do. Only with that clarity can you truly and genuinely differentiate yourself."

Do you see how the level-setting statement in each case sets the stage for a more compelling differentiator?

By stating the level-setting statement up front, you educate the other person about the industry you operate in, and establish a frame of reference that gives meaning to the differentiation that you want to communicate. You can use this technique to challenge an underlying assumption that people have about the industry, to illustrate a small but significant problem that generally annoys customers when dealing with your competitors, or anything else that allows you to highlight your solution.

Take a look at your own point of difference. Can you come up with a level-setting statement that will help you stand out even more?

Address the Stereotype Head-on

You know how as soon as people discover you're a [insert your title here], they immediately form an impression about you that's based on a stereotype?

Unfortunately, that stereotype is often negative.

You have two choices: you can use any of the other techniques listed here (and thereby delay telling them the usual job title that people typically recognize for your industry) or you can address the stereotype head-on and use it to your advantage. For professions such as life insurance agents or used car salespeople, where the negative stereotypes run strong and deep, I recommend you address the stereotype head-on:

"If I tell you that I'm a used car salesman, you're probably thinking 'plaid jacket guy who sells lemons to unsuspecting customers', right? Well, in fact, what I do is…"

Try it and watch them let their guard down!

The Straight Goods

"I'm a professional American civil war re-enactor and I often give keynotes as Abraham Lincoln." "I'm an astronaut training for a two-year mission on Mars." "I'm a psychic medium specializing in direct connections to Elvis."

When the work you do is inherently interesting, the best way to make people want to engage you in a conversation about it is to tell it exactly like it is!

So how do you know if what you do has inherent interest?

Easy. Go to networking events, ask your best customers, and let your passion for what you do show. Then let your impact statements, persuasion drivers and the responses you get be your guide. Remember, this isn't about adapting someone else's rule book or following a prescribed formula—it's about finding out what works best for you.

Now go out and have some conversations! As the saying goes, "If my mother never had a conversation with my father…'"

In sales as in courtship, think baby steps. You're not trying to tell your entire story, nor are you even trying to get the most important points out of your mouth first. All you want to accomplish is to elicit interest from the other person, to have that person say, "Tell me more."

Simple as it may seem, everything truly does start with a conversation.

Michel Neray

In the more than 25 years **Michel Neray** has been a communications professional, his successful approach has been based on the core question: "What's *your* Essential Message?" It has been the underlying principle of his work, first as an advertising copywriter, then as an entrepreneur making the rounds of the trade show circuit, as a sales and marketing executive, and now as president of The Essential Message.

Through his keynotes, workshops and coaching programs, Michel helps individuals and businesses discover their true differentiation and communicate it in the most compelling way. The Essential Message is like a unique selling proposition on steroids. More than just higher sales (as if that weren't enough!), clients and event participants say it gives them the confidence, resilience, and momentum that can only come from knowing who you are, the unique strengths that you bring to the table, and the true value you offer your customers and clients.

Thousands of entrepreneurs, independent professionals, and growing businesses have used The Essential Message to get the focus they need and the business they want. You can, too. Michel welcomes you to connect with him on FaceBook and Linkedin. For information about The Essential Message, or about having Michel speak at your event, please visit his website where you can also register to receive free "E-ssential Messages."

Michel has an undergraduate science degree from the University of Waterloo, and an MBA from McGill University. He is married with three children, two dogs, a sport motorcycle, a whitewater canoe and a second-degree black belt in Karate.

Business Name: Concentric Strategies Inc./The Essential Message
Address: 179 Strathearn Road, Toronto, ON M6C 1S3
Telephone: 416-782-4190
Email: themanager@essentialmessage.com
Web Address: www.EssentialMessage.com
Professional Affiliations: Canadian Association of Professional Speakers, International Federation for Professional Speakers

Carl D. Moore

The Associates, LLC

A.B.L.E. to Leap Tall Conflicts in a Single Bound!

>> The team is meeting to discuss a project. One member, Chris, is arguing to take the project in one direction and another person, Merrill, is arguing for a different direction. You and I are listening carefully to decide which one is superior. Suddenly, you and I notice that the pitch in Chris's voice has gone up just a bit and then the pitch in Merrill's voice also goes up a bit. A moment later, they are both yelling at one another. We're stunned and trying to understand what is happening. «

Emotionally tense moments, such as these, damage relationships and the effectiveness of teams. Everyone has experienced these moments. When I describe that simple conflict to an audience and ask them to describe what the rest of the people in the conference room are doing, everyone knows! The other people in the room are sitting quietly and uncomfortably, afraid to say anything for fear that the anger will be directed at them!

We are going to explore what is happening at a deeper level so we can understand how to change our behavior, how to avoid such moments, and even how to take effective control when heated conflict occurs. We may not change you into Superman or Superwoman, but we can make you A.B.L.E. to leap tall conflicts in a single bound!

A.B.L.E., of course, is an acronym:

- **A**ware of what is happening biologically and psychologically during emotionally tense moments;
- **B**ehavior counts, and monitoring your response to emotionally tense moments is paramount;
- **L**earn new behavioral responses to control emotionally tense moments;
- **E**xplore the other's "story" to understand the source of the conflict.

#1 Aware

The first step in the A.B.L.E. model is being **aware**—aware of what is happening biologically and psychologically when emotionally tense moments occur.

What Is Happening Biologically?

To understand better what is happening in our brain during these emotionally tense moments, neuroscientists in recent years have been using magnetic resonance imaging (MRI).[1] You've probably seen pictures of the brain taken with an MRI. It shows different parts of the brain in brilliant colors. The colors show the areas of the brain that are being activated and the degree to which they are being activated.

"Functional imaging" allows neuroscientists to create a movie of what is happening in the brain. It is referred to as an "fMRI." The researchers create an emotionally tense moment for the subject by showing, for example, threatening faces. In response to this simple threat, the researchers observe the blood flow in the brain as it was redirected away from the cortex and neo-cortex to the amygdala.

The cortex and neo-cortex are the portions of the brain that control such high-level functions as our mathematical and language skills and other forms of rational thought. When we are solving problems or focusing on communicating effectively, this part of the brain is engaged.

The amygdala is a small area at the base of the brain. It is one of the oldest, most primitive areas of our brain. Some neuroscientists refer to the amygdala as

---

1 E. A. Phelps, K. J. O'Connor, J. C. Gatenby, J. C. Gore, C. Grillon , & M. Davis (2001) "Activation of the left amygdala to a cognitive representation of fear," *Nature Neuroscience* 4, 437–441.

our "reptilian brain." That's how primitive it is! It controls our natural fear reaction. In short, the amygdala is where the ancient "fight or flight" response is located.

Stated another way, in that moment when an emotionally tense exchange is about to emerge, a moment when a person needs to be most intelligent, rational, and persuasive, the brain is literally dumbing the person down to the most primitive level!

You've had the experience of being involved in an emotionally tense exchange, and hours later or the next morning in the shower, it suddenly comes to you, "This is what I should have said! This is what I should have done!" The reason that you can't think of that great point or the perfect example in the moment is because the blood flow is going in the wrong direction! You are not thinking at all! You are literally on automatic pilot, driven by an emotional response that dates back to our prehistoric ancestors.

Except for the occasional tragic story in the news, this ancient "fight or flight" response does not actually appear as someone leaping across the conference table and strangling another. That would be a true "fight" response. Nor, when that shouting match erupts in the conference room, do the people at the table leap up and run screaming from the room. That would be real "flight." In the modern world, we understand that we are not really dealing with saber-toothed tigers; it's only our boss, colleague, customer, client, spouse, neighbor, or child. So the modern "fight or flight" reaction is modified. In today's world, here is how fight and flight translates:

1. **Fight:** A good word for this modified version of "fight" is "aggression" and this "aggression" shows itself as sarcasm, cynicism, ridicule, or other abusive behavior.

2. **Flight:** A good word to describe the modified version of "flight" is "regression." This "regression" shows itself as silence or people being frozen in place.

Return to that moment in the conference room. Everyone else is almost certainly frozen in place; afraid to say anything; not knowing what to say. The "aggression" of the two people in conflict is causing "regression" in the rest of the team.

It is very important to understand that the moment when a person becomes "aggressive" or when a person becomes "regressive," **neither feels safe**! When an emotional argument erupts and the rest of the team falls silent, it's relatively easy for me to look around the room and say to myself, "Ooh, they don't feel safe!"

However, when someone is in my face, yelling at me, it is very hard to say to myself, "Ooh, he doesn't feel safe!" It's almost impossible for me to think that simple truth because, in that moment, I am not feeling very safe and I am either going "aggressive" or "regressive" myself! My blood flow is going in the wrong direction for me to think the simple, coherent thought—"he's not feeling safe."

My challenge in that emotionally tense moment is to re-establish blood flow to my cortex and neo-cortex. We will consider how to accomplish that in a moment as we consider the next steps in the A.B.L.E. model. However, before getting to that solution, it is important to understand what is happening psychologically that makes this whole process even more complicated.

What Is Happening Psychologically?

Psychologists have a way of explaining how we take in information and process that information. It can be described in four progressive steps: 1) event, 2) facts, 3) story, and 4) reaction.

Understanding this process will help you understand how conflict arises between people. It will also give you a road map for understanding how to resolve conflict easily and naturally.[2]

Event	Facts	Story	Reaction
Something happens or there is an experience.	I select **facts** from the event or the experience.	I add **meaning**. I make **assumptions**. I draw **conclusions**. I tap into my **beliefs.**	I react **emotionally!**

---

2 Students of organizational development will recognize this process as the "Ladder of Inference," popularized by the work of Chris Argyris, and from Peter M. Senge, et al., *The Fifth Discipline Fieldbook: Strategies and Tools for Building a Learning Organization.* New York: Doubleday Dell Publishing Group, 1994. Students of psychology will recognize this as a variation on Rational Emotive Behavior Therapy, a form of Cognitive Behavior Therapy, which was first expounded by Dr. Albert Ellis in 1953.

The process begins with an **event.** Things are happening around us all the time. From any event, the human brain is designed to select **facts**. Imagine for a moment that there is a video camera suspended above your head with a wide-angle lens. That video camera is recording everything that is happening around you. Your brain is not designed to take in that much information. Your brain is designed to filter out much of the "noise" that goes on around you, so your brain very naturally and very automatically selects facts from everything going on around you. Then your brain constructs a **story** about those facts. The story has a number of elements. The story consists of *meanings* that you construe yourself and *assumptions* that you make about the *meanings*. You then draw *conclusions* based on the *meanings* and *assumptions,* and then these conclusions tie into *beliefs* that you hold. In turn, your beliefs then cause you to experience a **reaction.**

There are a number of things to understand in order to appreciate fully the implications of this function of our psychological habit of telling ourselves stories about what is happening around us. Let's begin by looking at how this process works in an everyday experience.

Road Rage!

You are driving down the road in heavy traffic. Suddenly, a car to your left cuts in front of you. The move is so instantaneous that it almost causes you to collide with this car. The car continues to the right lane and speeds up to accelerate beyond you. Those are the **facts** regarding this brief incident that your brain selects. Some people will take those facts and tell themselves a **story** about how dangerous that person is and they will slow down to give that person all the room he needs.

However, for some, the story will be very different. The story your brain starts to tell you could begin with *meaning* that might sound like this—"What a dangerous maneuver by that driver!" Your immediate *assumption* might be—"What an inconsiderate jerk!" Your conclusion might be—"I could have been seriously injured by that reckless idiot!" You have a strongly held belief about how you should be treated and you know—"I should never be treated in such a dangerous and inconsiderate way!" And this entire story—the meanings, assumptions, conclusions, beliefs—drives you to a strong, emotional **reaction**! You slam your foot on to the accelerator, you swerve into the open lane next to you, speed past that irresponsible idiot and cut in front of him to demonstrate that he cannot treat you in such a demeaning and disrespectful way!

That is what we call "road rage!" We'll return to road rage shortly, but first we should focus on three lessons that are important to understanding the role stories play in our daily lives.

Lesson #1—Lightening Fast!

It is important to understand that this **story** process is lightening fast. It is not a slow, rational, thoughtful process. It is a quick, emotional response. Think about the last time that you became really angry with someone. It was probably something very small that actually triggered your oversized response. It may have been a word, a tone of voice, a facial expression, or an attitude of being very dismissive toward you. Suddenly you were very upset! That moment is an example of the story process at work. It happens in the blink of an eye.

Lesson #2—Invisible!

When we get into conflict with others, our various **stories** are invisible to one another. When you become angry with a colleague because of a tone of voice or a word the colleague has used, the colleague has no idea where the anger is coming from. As with road rage, the story that the driver who cut you off is telling herself is invisible to you and your story is invisible to her.

The only way I can know someone else's story is to ask him. And the only way someone else can know my story is for me to tell him. We'll return to this concept of understanding the other's story later. For the moment, remember that the other person's story is invisible to me.

Lesson #3—We Never Overreact!

When there is an emotional explosion in a workplace, you will hear people talking about it later. They will say the person involved just "overreacted." Actually,

Awakening the Workplace

psychologists teach that we don't have a problem overreacting. Our reactions are exactly correct for the **stories** we have told ourselves. Our problem, according to the psychologists, is the exaggerated stories that we tell ourselves about the **facts** we have selected.

Let's return to the road rage example, which was a true story told by a National Public Radio (NPR) listener. In a program devoted to dealing effectively with stress in the modern world, the woman who called in to report her road rage wanted to explain how she had solved her road rage response. Her solution is exactly what psychologists say we have to do to change our behavioral reaction to emotionally tense moments. She *consciously changed* her story.

Instead of the story described above that got her angry and aggressive, she created a new story that kept her calm and even made her compassionate and empathetic! Her new story when someone cuts her off in traffic is, "Oh, that poor person! He must be very seriously ill and if he does not get to the hospital emergency room immediately, he is going to die!" Suddenly she is feeling compassion for the person who just cut her off.

The listener then acknowledged that her new story was very likely not the "truth." She said, "It's no truer than the story I was telling myself that got me so angry and stressed out and that made me a dangerous driver. My choice is between a story that stresses me out and makes me a hazard on the road or a story that keeps me cool, calm, and collected—and a safe driver." Which story do you think makes more sense?

Put in the context of the workplace, we often hear people talk about how a particular person makes them angry. The supervisor says that the employee's behavior, performance, or attitude makes her angry. The employee says that the supervisor's reaction or behavior makes him angry. In short, we routinely and automatically blame our emotional reaction on the other person when, in truth, what is making us angry, upset, or defensive is our own story about what is happening.

To summarize, when you become upset or angry with someone, it happens very quickly and you have no idea what the other's story is. The thing that gets you angry is your story about what is happening. In other words, our problem is our tendency to tell ourselves outrageous stories about other people's motives and intentions! Keep this in mind as we move to the second step in the A.B.L.E. model.

#2 Behavior

The second step in the A.B.L.E. model is **behavior** and it consists of two parts:

1. Decide that your behavior counts; that it is important to monitor and change your behavioral reaction to emotionally tense moments. Without such a resolution, you are stuck with your natural aggressive or regressive reaction.

2. Slow down your behavioral reaction in emotionally tense moments. Over 200 years ago, Thomas Jefferson wrote, "When angry, count to 10 before you speak." Jefferson then continued, "if very angry, a hundred." Jefferson understood that when a person is angry, he would—absolutely, positively, every single time—say things that will damage the relationship. If anger is addressed to someone with whom there is an ongoing relationship (employee, colleague, boss, spouse, significant other, child, neighbor), you now have two problems—the problem that started the disagreement and the damage now occurring to the relationship.

With what we now know from fMRIs about blood flow to the brain, it is clear why Jefferson's advice is so effective. In moments of mild agitation, it takes about 10 seconds to re-establish blood flow to the cortex and the neo-cortex. When a person is really agitated, it takes 10 times as long to re-establish the blood flow. In fact, neuroscientists also tell us, based on other work with fMRIs, that if we count to 10 in a foreign language, it more fully engages both hemispheres of our brain and makes it easier to re-establish blood flow to the cortex and neo-cortex. If you don't know a foreign language, go to the library and find out how to count to ten in your favorite foreign language—and then practice it! And practice leads to the third step in the A.B.L.E. model.

#3 Learn

The third step in the A.B.L.E. model is to **learn** a new behavioral response to emotionally tense moments. Recall that what is happening biologically in an emotionally tense moment is that the person who responds aggressively or regressively is not feeling safe! That is the trigger for the aggression or regression. You will find yourself in situations where it is not enough to simply monitor and control your own behavior by counting to 10 (or 100). You need to learn a new behavioral response that will help the other person, who is already in aggression, feel safe.

To accomplish this, you'll need a plan that is well rehearsed for dealing with these moments. Remember, your own blood flow may be going in the wrong direction so, unless you have a well-rehearsed plan of action, you may succumb to your own instinctual reaction (either aggression or regression). For a specific problem, you can create and rehearse a specific story, as in the road rage example. For other situations, you can create a more generic plan of response.

Creating Potential Responses

The following are two examples of approaches you can use to create and practice a new story for the situation.

Plan 1—Uninterrupted Listening

The first approach is simply remaining quiet and calm—having absolutely no response at all to the aggressive behavior of the other. It may seem like an eternity, and some very terrible and hurtful things may be said in those couple of minutes by the other person.

As you listen to this abusive tirade, your new story might be that you can also be this stupid and out of control! You must not take this personally, because if you do, you'll be sucked into an aggressive or regressive response. Once the tirade for the other subsides, take a deep breath and say something. The *something* you choose to say is the subject of the fourth and final step in the A.B.L.E. model—**explore**. Before going there, let's consider a second approach that you should plan and practice.

Plan 2—Develop a New Proactive Behavior

In some cases, it may be important to interrupt the emotional flooding of the other person in order to limit the damage and move to the final step in the A.B.L.E. model as quickly as possible. For example, as a supervisor, you may observe an emotionally tense moment erupt in front of you between two of your employees or between a customer and an employee. In such situations, you have a keen interest in limiting the damage by stopping the emotional flooding of one or both as quickly as possible. As the road rage discussion above illustrates, we have to create a new story for emotionally tense moments. Here are five important tips to use as you construct your new story:

1. Self-awareness: Quickly self-monitor your words, tone, and body language before you move into the role of assisting. If your words, tone, or body language are in any way aggressive, the other will react accordingly and you will aggravate the emotionally tense moment.

2. Identify the behavior: Name for yourself what you are observing, "This is anger," or "They are getting angry." Consciously saying to yourself what is happening and identifying the emotion helps you to maintain your calm.

3. Words, tone, body language: Spend some time thinking about a few words you can speak that you can always say in a calm and caring tone. For example, "I'm sorry; excuse me." If you know the name of the person who is emotionally flooding, say the person's name: "I'm sorry, John. Excuse me. John. I'm sorry." Repeating these words two or three times will stop the person's flooding in almost every situation.

Another example of calm, caring words are those that serve as "compliments" for the other person. One employee wants to stop the occasional rant by his supervisor. So, the employee rehearses a couple of sentences about how great this supervisor is to him. The next time the supervisor starts yelling at him, the employee takes a deep breath and begins to compliment the supervisor: "You are a great supervisor, one of the best supervisors I have ever had." After just a few sentences, the supervisor stops yelling and tries to figure out what the employee is talking about. The employee has stopped the supervisor's yelling and is now prepared to move to the final step in the A.B.L.E. model, which we will also do shortly.

4. Seal the "story": Add a powerful, positive emotion! Once you have created your new story for this emotionally tense moment, add a powerful emotion to your mental picture of this moment. For example, think about how empowering it will be for you to take control of emotionally tense moments effectively and turn them into relationship-building moments! The more powerful the positive emotion you create for this new skill, the more quickly this new story will take over and replace your old reaction to emotionally tense moments.

5. **Practice, practice, practice!** Once you have a clear image of your "new" reaction to emotionally tense moments, spend a few minutes a day rehearsing that new scene in your head. Visualize it clearly and powerfully! Within six weeks, you will see a significant change in your reaction to emotionally tense moments. (Note: If you don't experience a change, you may need some additional help. Take heed: sometimes deep-rooted issues can make it difficult for you to make this behavioral change. In that case, you may need to consult a professional and follow a prescribed plan. Tremendous advances are being made in this field; there is help!)

#4 Explore

The fourth and final step in the A.B.L.E. model is to **explore**. In the previous step, *learn*, you either listened quietly and patiently until the other's flooding ceased or you used the emotionally powerful new scene of your words, tone, and body language to stop the other's flooding. In either case, the other has stopped flooding and you are now ready for the final A.B.L.E. step: explore the other's story.

Exploring the other's story means fully listening for its facts and elements (meanings, assumptions, conclusions, and beliefs). It means listening:

- to hear with compassion (and not to argue or rebut);
- to truly understand every nuance in the other's story; and
- to behave as if this is your dearest friend in the whole world, and you want, more than anything, to understand the differences that exist between you.

Remember that this conversation can become emotionally tense very quickly. Remember how easily your story process can turn on; how quickly your own meanings, assumptions, conclusions, and beliefs can take over. The following is an example that you may experience:

A person you are speaking with says something that you think is completely wrong or misguided, and suddenly your story process kicks in with your own beliefs about what is happening. Instead of judging what the person just said based on your old story, you need to pause and calmly ask a question or make a comment, for example, "Can you help me understand why you think that?" or "I don't understand what leads you to believe that. Tell me more, please." By remaining calm, engaged, and neither aggressive nor regressive, you can make the other feel "safe" so that the conversation need never veer off into an emotional exchange.

Leaping Ahead

Do not deceive yourself. For most people, our natural reaction in emotionally tense moments is so hard-wired into our being that changing our reaction takes some work. Take heart! With a period of dedicated effort, you can change your automatic response to emotionally tense moments. When you do, your effectiveness in the workplace, and in your personal relationships, will be dramatically improved. You may not really be Superman or Superwoman, but you will be A.B.L.E. to leap tall conflicts in a single bound!

Carl D. Moore, Esq.

Carl Moore is an employment attorney. After 25 years in employment litigation, serving as an attorney for management, a union and as a neutral, he was selected by George Mitchell and Robert Dole, US Senate majority and minority leaders, to create and administer the first EEO complaint process for Senate employees. In the Senate, Carl trained more than 1,300 managers and employees in a wide range of human resources and equal employment opportunity issues.

Prior to his service in the Senate, Carl designed and taught a course for the Department of Justice. Through that course, he trained more than 1,800 government attorneys in employment law. Carl was the principal co-author of the first textbook that covered all of US Federal civil service employment law (*Civil Service Law and Procedure: A Basic Guide*, BNA, 1984 and 1991). His degrees are from Texas Tech University and the University of Texas Law School.

Business Name:	The Associates, LLC
Address:	PO Box 136, Orlean, VA 20128
Telephone:	703-606-1796
Email:	carl@carlmoore.com
Web Address:	www.carlmoore.com
Professional Affiliations:	Texas Bar Association, Bar of the District of Columbia, National Speakers Association

Behold this day! It is yours to make.

Black Elk, Oglala Sioux Medicine Man

Susan Stewart

Live Well, Laugh Lots

Creating Dynamics for Team Success

You cannot become successful, you can only be successful.

Eckhart Tolle, *A New Earth*

What Is Success, Anyway?

Success is a word that has been traditionally used when a person or a team achieves what they set out to do and the end result is an abundance of money, power, or status. Yet, the meaning of success is beginning to evolve. There is now a growing understanding that success is not something you can acquire and it certainly can't be achieved at all costs. What many are realizing is that success is a *state of being* that we can choose. When we are passionate about what we do and filled with joy as we work toward our goals, we are successful. Similarly, team success occurs when everyone on the team is giving it their all and positive energy flows among its members. Strong effort combined with positive dynamics is the ultimate performance goal for a team, and that combination inevitably leads to exciting outcomes.

When it comes to being successful, it's not about the things that you do, but rather, the person you are.

Marianne Williamson (as quoted on
"Oprah & Friends" on XM Radio)

Good Teams Versus High Performance Teams

It's quite easy to be a good team. All you need to be a good team is to have intelligent, experienced, and capable team members. A good team has solid technical ability that produces results that will do just fine, thank you very much. However, to be a high performance team requires taking that technical ability and combining it with "intangibles" that you cannot see or measure. The intangibles on the team exist when you have team members who constantly interact with each other with kindness, positivity, compassion, and respect. High performance teams have an overall energy you can feel by how positive the dynamics are among the members.

> *Becoming less attached to outcomes doesn't mean that you*
> *don't care or that you don't try. Instead, it's more a matter*
> *of trying really hard, caring a great deal, and putting the*
> *odds in your favor.*
>
> Richard Carlson, PhD, *Don't Sweat the*
> *Small Stuff and It's All Small Stuff*

High performance teams separate themselves from the good teams by doing one main thing; that is, they focus on their performance rather than outcomes. This is not to say that high performance teams don't work towards their goals; they most certainly do. However, they spend all of their energy on making the team as strong as possible (their performance), which naturally creates the outcomes they desire. How many teams have you been on throughout your career that spent almost all of their energy focusing on the end result and neglected their quality of performance? Focusing on performance is based on the choices that the team members make on a daily basis. These include:

- Knowing that the dynamics among them are the foundation for their success;
- Putting forth effort toward the goal one hundred percent of the time;
- Interacting and decision making that flows from having the success of the team in mind, rather than individual egos;
- Regarding mistakes or setbacks as steps to success rather than catastrophes;
- Seeing the immense value of work–play balance.

>> Bill Tschirhart is the former national development coach for the Canadian Curling Association, the former provincial coach for British Columbia, and currently a competitive consultant for the World Curling Players Association. (And he is also my father.) Bill has coached many of the world's top curling teams. Almost every time a team has flown him out to their city to work with them, it hasn't been because they need help with their curling deliveries or brushing skills, but rather, because the "engine light" has gone on—the dynamics among the players have weakened and they need help getting back on track with each other.

After many years of the same kind of phone calls from high performance curling teams, Bill has drawn this conclusion: "Regardless of the perceived problems a team might have, it almost always (90 percent of the time) relates to some aspect of team dynamics."

"When I reflect on my years as a competitive curler and the teams on which I've been a member, each unsuccessful season (we weren't passionate about making it to the provincials AND didn't have much fun trying) can be directly linked to issues surrounding the energy between the members. We were always four reasonably good curlers, but we were always four reasonably good curlers who didn't have the positive dynamics among us to create the outcomes we desired." <<

To understand the significant impact that team dynamics have on performance, think back to the problems or issues you've had on a project team, or in a unit or branch. Ask yourself, "Was it because of something technical (a lack of knowledge, lack of resources, lack of organization, for example) or did it have something to do with a lack of commitment, honest communication, trust, accountability, or positive energy?"

Five Dynamics of a High Performance Team

There are five key dynamics that high performance teams consistently have and that make them successful. Keep in mind that team dynamics are extremely interconnected so if one (or more) dynamic is lacking on the team, the chances of the team having the other dynamics are slim to none. For optimal interactions to make a team successful, it's pretty much an all or nothing scenario. These five essential dynamics of high performance teams are:

1. Similar level of commitment and effort;
2. Accountability and honest communication;
3. Encouragement of and belief in each other;
4. Positive energy and humor;
5. Trust.

#1—Similar Level of Commitment and Effort

Teams are like a committed relationship or marriage. For a team to work really well, everyone needs to be equally enthusiastic about being there, while expending the same amount of energy to reach the desired level of performance. One of the most effective conversations a team can have (ideally when it forms, when a new member joins, or at the beginning of a new task/project) is a discussion that results in everyone agreeing to what the team's goals are and being on the same page in terms of striving for those goals.

However, the communication regarding the expected commitment and effort must be open and honest. It's a disaster when, to be accepted by the team, someone only says what he/she feels the other members of the team want to hear. Sooner or later, that team member will be unhappy and not working at the performance level of the others. When each team member has the same vision of success and clearly understands the performance level that is required to get there, that reduces potential misunderstanding down the road. Many times on a team, there will be varying degrees of effort put forth by its members, which stems from the team not having a unified definition of success. An abundance of harmony, which is a precious commodity on a team, can exist when everyone is on the same "wavelength" and demonstrates the same level of passion.

#2—Accountability and Honest Communication

For those times when one or more members of the team aren't on the same page as everyone else in terms of performance level, it takes accountability and honest communication to get everyone back on track and to regain focus.

» For example, a member of the team is less than thrilled about the expectations involved in a new project. After a week of saying and emailing negative comments about the project, the team calls a meeting to address the issue. As each person shares his or her concerns regarding the negative energy, the team member listens to what is being said and then apologizes for the behavior and promises to adjust his attitude towards the project to help everyone stay focused. «

Here's a great example of the team members putting their egos aside for the greater good of the team. Most people find it extremely difficult to take ownership for an error or be upfront with someone, but admitting one's errors or getting things off one's chest are the only ways the team can truly be unified. When a team member doesn't accept responsibility for something they've done or not done, the other team members begin to doubt if that team member truly cares about the team, and that doubt can easily build into such lower energies as anger, frustration, and resentment.

Those same low energies can arise when team members don't talk honestly with each other when something happens that upsets someone or hinders the team's performance. The exact opposite of honest communication is silence, and when feelings go unsaid, low energies fester inside the team. You can have a great team with oodles of technical ability, but the moment someone doesn't admit to something, or the members start carrying around a silent grudge, the team's ability to perform at a high level comes to a grinding halt.

» I have lost many curling games or gone through a disappointing curling season because of unspoken tension between two or more players on the team. There have been many examples throughout my competitive curling career when we had the game lost even before stepping on to the ice. Many lessons have been learned about the extreme importance of "having it out" with each other and then moving on. How can a team perform at a high level when some of the members can only see red? «

Honest communication is one of the most critical yet most difficult team dynamics to have in place. This is one of the toughest actions for a member to take because of the "F-word"—fear that is, which stems from our almighty egos. Keep in mind that our ego is the identification we give ourselves based on our thoughts. There is an ongoing desire to protect our ego by protecting the thoughts we have about ourselves. If we feel that our ego (the thoughts we have about ourselves) is under attack, we avoid the person or situation that is putting it at risk.

Fear is one of the major hindrances to the potential success of an organization and the teams within it. Any time conflict or negativity occurs in the workplace or on a team, it's because deep down the people involved are scared of something and are protecting their sense of self. Fear is what can block teams from becoming high performance, because the team members are expending a great deal of energy protecting their sense of self (ego) rather than building their sense of team.

To achieve the challenging dynamic of accountability and honest communication, the team must release its collective fears connected to failure. If you are interested in building accountability and honest communication on a current or future team, create a positive culture surrounding failures or mistakes—help the team see them as moments of profound learning and growth rather than sheer disasters. When teams view mishaps and setbacks as being purposeful steps to success, everyone feels safer in taking risks and talking honestly with each other.

#3—Encouragement of and Belief in Each Other

The branch that takes care of recruitment, health and safety, and learning in an organization is called "Human Resources" and not "Robot Resources." Use this to remind yourself that there are humans (a.k.a. emotional beings) on teams and that humans can easily be distracted by and attach themselves to negative energy. If a team member feels or knows that her peers are doubting her abilities and/or talking behind her back, then her focus can easily go from productive to destructive as she starts spending her precious time and energy worrying about what is being said about her rather than doing all she can to help the team. All teams will move closer to being successful by waking up and realizing how damaging negative energy can be and how powerful positive affirmations truly are.

**The dynamic of encouragement and belief in each other is
achieved quite simply when the team members are aware of
how effective it is to have a positive energy flowing among
them and helping everyone to stay the course.**

Again, if everyone has agreed to the goal(s) and has agreed to be on the same
page to get there, why would you distract a team member and weaken the team's
performance?

#4—Positive Energy and Humor

*I attract to my life whatever I give my attention, energy, and
focus to, whether positive or negative.*

Michael J. Losier, *The Law of Attraction*

Consider that everything and everyone on our planet has energy, and according to
that energy, everything and everyone vibrates at a certain level. For humans, our
energy is created by the thoughts and feelings we have, including the comments
we make. Here's the negative chain reaction: *negative feelings create negative
energy, and negative energy puts out low vibrations*. Here's the positive chain reaction: *positive feelings create positive energy, and positive energy puts out high
vibrations*. Everyone gives off vibrations or, as we tend to say, "vibes," and those
vibrations (whether negative or positive) are pushed out, matched, and delivered
right back to us in the form of experience—this is what is called *the law of attraction*. Whether you are focusing on something that creates negative feelings in you
or positive ones, the law of attraction simply matches your vibrations and gives you
more of the same. Understanding the law of attraction can assist teams immensely.
All teams will get closer to being successful when they become aware of their
thoughts and comments (their energy) because they understand that the team's
energy creates the team's experience. Think about when you have had a string of
great days and then said, "I'm on a roll!" Because your energy creates your experience, you were indeed! Well, have you ever had a string of rotten days and then
said, "I'm on a roll"? Probably not, but you were indeed! Our energy is extremely

powerful and it can work to our advantage or it can be something that blocks us from experiencing success. Do you know someone who seems to "have it all"? They've got the great career, strong marriage, gorgeous home, adorable children, large income, fabulous vacations, and the kicker is that they are positive! Consider that their positive energy was there long before they "had it all," and apply that same scenario to your team. Raise the energy of the team and you are raising the experience of the team.

#5—Trust

Trust is usually the main focus of a team-building session because it is the main indicator of the team's overall dynamics. To put it quite simply, trust is achieved on a team when all the members have the feeling that everyone is doing their *very best* to help the team be successful, and if everyone is doing their very best, chances are you have the other four key dynamics in place. On the flip side, when there is an element of complacency on the team, this brings about mistrust. Think about how trusting you are of your team members when you have that feeling in your gut that they couldn't care less how the team performs or how the project turns out. It's pretty hard to trust that person or feel as if you can go to them for help, right? Now, think about how trusting you are and eager to chat with your team members when you feel that they are firing on all cylinders. Those two scenarios are like night and day and dictate whether the team is merely good or performing at a high level.

Trust is also built when the leader is passionate about the team. When a leader "walks the talk," is enthusiastic about the team's missions, and makes everyone feel that their role is vital, there is naturally more trust on the team. It's really hard to be inspired and put out 100 percent when your leader is merely going through the motions. The final element to trust is through self-empowerment. When each team member has the belief that they are an integral part of the whole when it comes to the team's success, they show up every day and do their very best.

> If you want something that you've never had before, you must
> be prepared to do things you've never done before.
> > Bill Tschirhart, World Curling Players Association

Building Positive Team Dynamics

Since we've reviewed the five key dynamics of high performance teams, you might be thinking, *"How the heck do we get there from here?"* There are many methods to improve the dynamics on the team, yet it all starts with talking to each other. For many teams out there, this will be a large adjustment as the number of "elephants" in the room makes it hard to move about sometimes. Like saving a marriage, getting it all out on to the table is ground zero and absolutely necessary if things are to improve. However, for communication to be successful, it must be done in a safe and respectful way. Consider the following four methods to get everyone talking more and removing the anxiety around it:

1. Stop-Start-Continue: This is a very effective way to have each team member evaluate the dynamics of the team and clearly communicate how to improve them. Give each team member their own piece of paper and have them make three columns on it. The first column is entitled "STOP," the second column "START," and the third column "CONTINUE." In the first column, they will list all the things they would like to see the team stop doing; in the second, all the things they would like to see the team start doing; in the third, all the things they feel are working just fine and that the team should celebrate. After everyone is done the exercise, a nominated team member will read the lists anonymously, or if everyone feels comfortable with it, each member can read their list to the rest of the team. Keep in mind that any team member can call a STOP-START-CONTINUE meeting and it can be done as many times as necessary throughout the life of the team. S-S-C is best done on a regular basis as a proactive tool to prevent team dynamics issues from arising in the first place.

2. Form a Communication Policy: One of Canada's most successful women's curling teams was Team Sandra Schmirler. They had such a large respect for the link between honest communication and high performance that the four players made it a policy that if anyone on the team had something to say to another team member or another player, they had a specific number of hours to find the time to sit down and talk to them. The Schmirler team's policy also stated that after the discussion took place, all players involved were to put it behind them and *move on*.

Susan Stewart

Establishing a communication policy on a team reduces the occurrence of team members dragging unexpressed resentment and anger around with them regarding a situation that took place days, weeks, or months ago. The "letting go" part of the policy is right on the mark, as well, when it comes to retaining focus on the job at hand. The healthiest conflict is caught (soon after the incident) and released because there are bigger fish to fry.

3. Discuss the "Wins" as Often as the "Losses": Typically, teams only evaluate things and communicate honestly with each other when trouble is on the horizon or it has already hit. When teams only reflect with each other when issues or problems arise, that pattern can create a negative association with communication. Meetings in the workplace can cause some people to go into fear mode because that usually means something has gone wrong. Consider gathering the team after something went really well and talk about why the team was successful. Having the team talk honestly about what the team did right not only creates a more positive association with communication, but it also generates a great checklist of things that the team can refer back to as a general set of performance goals.

> *Trust is built when there is a combination of equal effort and empathy. The better we know each other, the greater the chance we will empathize.*
>
> Kate Koppett, *Training to Imagine*

4. Laugh, Play, and Get to Know Each Other: Building positive dynamics within a team can also be achieved by instilling the value of work–play balance. The five key dynamics previously addressed have a much greater chance if the team *shares* moments of laughter, has *fun* together, and gets to *know each other* beyond the scope of the workplace. When teammates experience fun together and share things about their lives, they will not only have a more unified spirit, but they will simply be more comfortable with being accountable and honest with each other in the future. One of the most effective things a team can do is to integrate laughter and fun into their journey because that is a significant part of success. It raises the overall energy of the team (remember the law of attraction!) and it translates into a stronger overall performance.

» As an employee of a human resources branch in the Ontario Public Service, I worked in a smaller organizational planning and development unit with three other vibrant women and we had a strong culture of work–play balance. The four of us got to know things about each other that went beyond the walls of the workplace. Our team worked hard but balanced that effort with having fun inside and outside of the workplace. Throughout the years we spent working together, not a day went by that we didn't share at least one good laugh. It's because we had so many memories of having a good time together that positive team dynamics came naturally to us. «

Don't expect (or fear) that your team will become like the "*Ya-Ya Sisterhood*" or a championship-winning sports team spraying each other with champagne. However, consider how much easier those five dynamics of success will be to instill or enhance if your team fosters a culture of lightheartedness and fun. Humor and work–play balance are key to success because the team is *enjoying the journey as much as working towards the goal*. Stand back and ask yourself how much work–play balance exists on your team. Consider to what degree your team looks at the process as a means to an end and if they can't wait for it all to be over because they're all barely hanging on. If achieving the goal sucks the soul out of everyone and leaves them gasping for air, can you truly call that a *success*?

Knowing Is Not the Hard Part

Most of the information you just read about team dynamics, you already knew instinctively. You are simply being reminded that it takes more than technical ability to be a successful team. It's now time to move to action, as *the knowing* is not the hard part when it comes to having strong team dynamics—it's *the doing*. Being a successful team is about experiencing a balance of effort and joy, an awareness of the "intangibles" on the team, and an acceptance that the overall team energy will truly raise the level of performance and lead the team to its goals.

Susan Stewart

Inspirational speaker **Susan Stewart** is both a recovering stand-up comic and a former learning and development consultant. After performing stand-up comedy across Canada for five years, Susan found herself employed in a Human Resources branch within the Ontario Public Service (long story).

While working on a wellness initiative, Susan decided to get back on stage and use her comedic powers for good rather than evil! Susan has since developed light-hearted workshops and powerful keynote presentations that lead people to create habits that match their desires and experience successful working relationships. Since 2005, Susan Stewart has been delivering her smash-hit presentations on wellness, work–life balance, humor, positive energy, team dynamics and the powers of improvisation.

Business Name: Live Well, Laugh Lots
Address: 1233 Yonge Street, #306, Toronto, ON M4T 1W4
Telephone: 416-828-0064
Email: susanstewart64@mac.com
Web Address: www.susanstewart.ca
Speaking Affiliations: Canadian Association of Professional Speakers

Favorite Quotation:
And the day came, when the risk to remain tight and in a bud was more painful than the pain it took to blossom.

                                                    Anaïs Nin

Joanne Steed-Takasaki

JOSTA Consulting, Inc.

Shifting Gears: Stress Management Tools to Put You Back in the Driver's Seat

Several years ago, a colleague of mine joked with me about all the life challenges I had recently faced and how I had moved through them. My colleague informed me that I needed to develop some bad habits in order to cope. She was worried about me because I didn't drink, smoke, overeat, shop obsessively, or exhibit any other behavior she felt would help me manage my stress. We had a good laugh, but the conversation got me thinking about what I was doing to cope with my challenges, and how others around me handled their challenges differently than I did.

Looking back, I realize that even before I started my serious research on stress management, I had already utilized some successful strategies. From this early awareness about stress, coupled with research and teaching, I've developed an approach that puts *you* in the driver's seat to de-stressing your life. We'll look at some of this research about stress, and then focus on a five-point model that is easy to integrate into a busy life.

The Body and Stress

Stress is definitely not something new. In 1932, Walter B. Cannon, a physiologist at the Harvard Medical School, described the body's reaction to stress, and in 1956, Dr. Hans Selye of the University of Montreal was able to specify the physiological changes in the body due to stress. Selye recognized the need for people and society to make informed choices about handling the stresses of life. Since then, many researchers have turned their attention to stress. All of us, and especially those of us in professions known for high levels of stress and burnout, have an obligation to find out more about this important subject.

How do we go about this? How do we begin to handle this thing we call stress that tears through our emotions, causes discomfort in our relationships, and depletes our immune system? Paula Jorde Bloom, in her book *Avoiding Burnout: Strategies for Managing Time, Space, and People in Early Childhood Education*, wrltes:

> Our challenge in managing stress…is to gain as many insights as possible into the correlation between stress and performance in our own lives. Only then can we begin to re-engineer our behavior and our environment to use stress to our advantage, benefiting from its positive aspects while minimizing its negative ones.

Our Need for "Eustress"

Overall, stress is receiving bad publicity. We seem to hear only about stress in a negative context. It is valuable to understand that we each need some stress to lead a successful and challenging life. Stress that produces personal growth, or spurs us on to accomplish our goals is called eustress, a term coined by Hans Selye. Eustress is "good stress." And it serves several important purposes. Stress is a protector and gives us a mechanism for dealing with threats. It provides us with the adrenaline necessary to play sports, write exams, and follow our passions and dreams. Stress adds anticipation and excitement to our lives. T. Harv Eker, in his book *Mastering the Secrets of the Millionaire Mind*, states that, "Being comfortable may make us feel warm and fuzzy, but it doesn't allow us to grow. The only time you are actually growing is when you are out of your comfort zone." And stress definitely nudges—or in some cases yanks—us out of our comfort zone.

One of my passions is working in the fitness industry, and as a personal trainer, I see the positive effects of stress continually. If an individual wants to increase their muscle size, they must apply resistance to that muscle in order for it to grow. If they want to enhance their cardiovascular system, it must be stressed in order to progress. However, this stress needs to be carefully planned in order to have maximum benefits. Just the right amount of stress can create beautiful biceps! Too much stress or overtraining, however, can have negative effects on the body. Similarly, you do not grow "emotional or intellectual biceps" without resistance or adversity. And similarly, too much stress or adversity without proper coping techniques can also have adverse effects on you.

The Stress Response

In understanding stress, it is important to have a fundamental knowledge of the way our bodies respond to stress. In the 1920s, Walter B. Cannon established the "fight or flight" description of stress. Simply put, when we encounter stress in our lives, our sympathetic nervous system immediately prepares for "fight or flight," through creating such bodily responses as an increased heart rate, increased sugar and fat levels, reduced intestinal movement, dilated pupils, increased perspiration, decreased blood clotting time, and constricted blood vessels. (The sympathetic nervous system could be compared to the gas pedal in your car.) Primitively, we would have run away from or fought our stress enemy, and this expelled energy would have caused our parasympathetic nervous system (the brakes) to take over and return our bodies to homeostasis.

Modern stressors, however, are often psychological rather than physical, but our bodies do not make this distinction. Therefore, our sympathetic nervous system activates our stress response when things go wrong at work, at home, or in our relationships. As our body is designed to react to stress physically—say by running away or fighting the enemy—our parasympathetic nervous system does not activate and our body remains stuck in a hyper-vigilant state. Over time, the repeated activation of the stress response, without moving to action followed by homeostasis, takes a heavy toll on the body. It can cause damage to our cardiovascular systems, suppress our immune systems, and actually increase our vulnerability to everyday pressures and mental problems. Researchers now believe that most, if not all, illnesses are related to unrelieved stress.

The goal to maintaining health is to find ways to activate our parasympathetic nervous system and bring our bodies back to homeostasis when dealing with our stressful lives. Achieving a better balance in life is the key. Let's look at a five-part model that contributes to achieving balance:

1. Intellectually/cognitively;
2. Physically;
3. Emotionally;
4. Behaviorally; and
5. Spiritually.

#1—Intellectual/Cognitive Balance

The most powerful tool you can bring on board to help with your stress reduction is your mind. An intellectual understanding of stress involves both an understanding of the physiological stress response and a plan to combat the effects of stress in your life. Your thoughts have a profound impact on how stress affects you.

It starts with *how* you see a stressful event, because how you perceive a situation can trigger the stress response. The bottom line is that you are not stressed until you have a stressful thought. Thought processes, whether positive or negative, optimistic or pessimistic, determine stress levels and, ultimately, your actions and reactions to what is occurring in your world.

For example, these Ds—difficulty, disappointment, discouragement, despair, and divorce—are powerful teachers. They can teach empathy, build character, and strengthen resolve if we allow them to. Shortly after the death of my parents, I sat on the couch crying and wondering, "What do I do with all this pain?" Well, the answer came to me days later…use it! With a new resolve, I converted the pain to inspiration to make changes in my life and used it as the motivator to help others—both ways of using this challenge as a power for good.

Much has been written about the power of our thoughts in recent years. Taking the time to analyze our thinking, and the incredible power it has in our lives, can literally change our lives. In fact, if we do not change our thinking, we cannot change our lives.

Three Steps to More Empowering Thoughts

1. Be aware of your thoughts and emotions: If your mind is a bad neighborhood to be in, move out and find a new place to live! Awareness is the key to changing your stressful thinking patterns. Once you are aware of your negative thoughts, make the choice to stay away from toxic individuals, situations, and places that will increase your negative thinking. Avoid "water-cooler workshops." The negativity of co-workers can take you away from your own dreams and passions, and drag you down into workplace gossip and backbiting.

2. Thoughtfully list your goals and dreams: With no holds barred, write down what you would do if you weren't afraid to fail. Believe in yourself and your abilities to make your dreams come true. How does this help reduce stress? Having a vision, a passion, and a focus will help to bring stressful situations into perspective.

3. Allow only thoughts of optimism and success in your mind: Reframe negative experiences and find the positive in everything that life throws at you. Change the rules for happiness that you have created in your mind. Remember those goals you listed? Find ways of making your stressful situations help you make those dreams come true. That stressful co-worker and overbearing boss are serving a purpose. They may be moving you closer to your goals or teaching you what *not* to do when you are the boss of your own business or teaching you the patience to be a better parent, spouse, or friend.

#2—Physical Balance

One of my passions is working in the fitness industry. It is the greatest of joys to guide the transformation of people's minds, bodies, and lives as they incorporate regular physical activity into their stressful, overbooked lives. A fitness center is like my own "stress lab." I see patrons come in with the weight and stress of work and life written in their faces and carried in their bodies, and leave with that weight lifted and a renewed focus and energy to carry on.

The benefits of regular exercise are numerous and vary from person to person. Of course, the health benefits are universal; lowering your risk of heart attack, strengthening your bones, and decreasing your risk of diabetes are among the most important. However, patrons I speak to mention things like increased self-esteem, increased strength, feeling healthier, sleeping better, controlling weight, looking good, reducing stress, providing time for self, and improving attitude and outlook as their personal rewards for making the time to exercise.

It is important to realize that making time to exercise does not need to involve working out in an intimidating gym environment with a bunch of muscle heads. (Although a personal trainer can give you the knowledge to turn that intimidating gym into your playground!) Recreational sports, walking the dog, jogging, parking further away from your destination, and using the stairs can all be great ways to get you off the couch and on your way to physical fitness.

Along with physical exercise, it is essential to incorporate proper nutrition into your lifestyle. Not only is food one of life's pleasures, it also fuels our bodies and helps maintain overall health. My food recommendations are always quite simple. Try not to let yourself get too hungry. Hunger depletes the energy you need to make wise food choices. Instead of eating two or three large meals, eat five or six small meals a day. Eat a balanced diet with a variety of foods that will provide you with the six basic nutrients of health: carbohydrates, fat, protein, vitamins, minerals, and water. Following the Canada Food Guide or the USDA Food Pyramid will put you on the right path.

Three Steps to Achieving Physical Balance

1. Choose a physical activity you enjoy: Choosing the right physical activity is essential. Your choice of activity will depend on what you are interested in, your schedule, your need to be with people or alone, and your main goals for exercise.

2. Write down your goals: Remember, a goal is just a wish until you write it down. Be specific. Make schedules. Set deadlines. Outline the important benefits and rewards you will receive from exercise. Display your goals where you are regularly able to see them.

3. Have the courage and commitment to carry out your plan: Make sure you have built in accountability—have a friend go walking with you, join a recreation league with your co-workers, have an accountability partner you report to weekly, or hire a personal trainer to make you accountable at the gym.

#3—Emotional Balance

When former First Lady of the United States, Barbara Bush, addressed the graduating students at Wellesley College, she counseled:

> *As important as your obligations as a doctor, lawyer, or business leader will be, you are a human being first, and those human connections— with your spouses, with children, with friends—are the most important investments you will ever make. At the end of your life, you will never regret not having passed one more test, not winning one more verdict, or not closing one more deal. You will regret time not spent with a husband, a child, a friend, or a parent.... Our success as a society depends not on what happens in the White House but on what happens inside your own house.*

When I speak about emotional balance, I am not referring to keeping emotions in check, showing no fear, or expressing no feelings. A common myth in our society is that to be successful, one must be tough and invulnerable. In fact, I define emotional balance as making the time to develop and cultivate successful, fulfilling relationships in our lives where we can find a place of security in which we can express our emotions, our fears and our vulnerabilities, and truly be ourselves. These relationships provide a shelter from the stresses of the world. They provide a place where creativity can flourish, and a place where gratitude and hope are carefully nourished.

In our overscheduled and frantic society, looking after our emotional balance can be a challenge. Developing mutually supportive relationships and friendships takes time and effort, and is often set aside for more demanding tasks at work. Developing and cultivating a social support network is essential for a healthy mind and body. Loved ones, business associates, neighbors, and pets can all provide emotional balance. My husband and I have two adorable Yorkshire terriers. I'm quite sure just looking at these fluffy little dust mops lowers my blood pressure and brings a smile to my face. The research agrees with me. Pets have been found to reduce blood pressure and levels of stress hormones, improve chances of survival after life-threatening illness, provide companionship, promote social responses, and enrich lives.

>> The most powerful force in my journey for emotional balance has been gratitude. Several years ago, my mother and father died just several months apart. My mother died of cancer and my father was struggling with Alzheimer's. Both of these diseases take heavy tolls on the caregivers. Shortly after their deaths, my son moved away to college, and then my daughter moved 21 hours from home to attend university. I was dealing with a great deal of loss over a very short time. At a particularly frustrating time in my daughter's first year away, we established a ritual of emailing each other every morning and ending the email by expressing what we are grateful for that day. We end with the line, "I am grateful for…" «

This started as a tool to help my daughter, but the benefits on a personal level have been monumental. It is amazing how that simple ritual has transformed our lives, and strengthened our relationship. On difficult days, we have found that no matter how bad the day might be, there are always many things that are going right, and many things to be grateful for. It is interesting that our mood can be transformed instantly by listing our blessings in an expression of gratitude.

If we are feeling discouraged, it is because we have forgotten
or suppressed all the reasons we could be feeling happy.
And conversely, if we are feeling good,
it is because we are not dwelling on all the reasons
we could be feeling discouraged. It's just that simple.

While carrying out research for my master's degree, I became fascinated with the topic of hope. A few months prior to my returning to university, I had watched my mom wage an 18-month battle against ovarian cancer, and saw the physical and emotional difference that her unwavering hope and faith made in the quality of her life during this difficult time. I soon became a firm believer in the importance of hope in our lives. Jevne, Nekolaichuk, and Boman (1999)[1] ask:

What is this thing called hope? We ridicule those with too much of it. We hospitalize those with too little. It is dependent on so many things, yet indisputably necessary to most. Those with it live longer. Words can destroy it. Science has neglected it. A day without it is dreadful. A day with an abundance of it guarantees little.

Margaret Sommerville answers this question beautifully by saying, "Hope is the oxygen of the human spirit." Of course, none of us can live without oxygen.

Three Steps to Achieving Emotional Balance

1. **Incorporate genuine gratitude into your life**: When the alarm rings in the morning, instead of immediately starting a dialogue of negativity about how tired you still are, how you hate your work, and so on, just say, "Thank you." Start listing all the positive things you have in your life. Be grateful for the day and the many opportunities you will be able to create through your gratitude and happiness.

2. **Develop mutually loving and supportive relationships**: Fiercely protect your connections to those you care most about, eliminate the toxic relationships you are currently involved in, and free yourself to start a new life of optimism and joy. Create or focus on enhancing at least one essential relationship, whether it is a friend, a family member, or a pet. Even watching your fish will lower your blood pressure and calm your mind (however, they are never quite the same after you take them out for an afternoon walk!).

3. **Have hope!** Make a conscious choice to begin practicing hope. Look for hope in all you do, and in all you see. Listen to the voices of hope in those around you, and in the experiences of others. Borrow hope from others when your "hope supply" is low, and freely lend it to others when your supply is strong. Find hope in laughter, in nature, in adversity, in suffering, in happiness. Hope is all around us if we just choose to experience it.

---

1 "Experiments in Hope: Blending Art and Science with Service." Published by the Hope Foundation of Alberta: <www.ualberta.ca/HOPE>.

#4—Behavioral Balance

We all have some strategies in place to deal with our stress. Strategies are those behaviors that we carry out in an attempt to reduce the stress we are feeling in our lives. There are both beneficial and detrimental strategies. Detrimental strategies are those that may temporarily reduce our stress, but have long-term negative effects. Many of our stress management strategies involve some type of "self-medication." For example, caffeine, a stimulant found in coffee, some soft drinks, and chocolate, chemically induces the fight or flight response in our bodies and can actually end up increasing our daily stress. Alcohol consumption, drug abuse, and blaming others may make us feel better temporarily, but will cause more stress in the long run.

Beneficial strategies involve making behavior changes that will have long-term positive effects on our stress. Developing skills in organization and time management are behaviors that are key components in reducing stress. Stephen Covey, in his book *The Seven Habits of Highly Effective People,* tells us that "'time management' is really a misnomer—the challenge is not to manage time, but to manage ourselves." There will always be more things to do in a day than we have time for. A first step in managing our time better is to take the time to assess how we are presently spending our time. Divide your day into 15-minute segments and review your time spent on various activities throughout the day. Evaluate your use of time, and decide on changes and adjustments that can be made. Prioritize and make sure you take care of the important things first. Then add in less important tasks.

Taking time to set short-, medium-, and long-term goals will help you to have a clear sense of where you want to go. Making lists each day can help you accomplish more and give you the means to get to where you want to go. Remember: procrastination is the enemy. It is responsible for much of the stress, disappointment, and frustration that we feel. So, get rid of the excuses, limit the interruptions, get off the couch, and do what needs to be done.

Clean up your workspace, organize your files, and put everything in its place. This simple (or perhaps not so simple) exercise can "de-clutter" your mind and improve the efficiency of your work. Releasing ourselves from clutter and confusion can bring new clarity to the challenges and problems we are dealing with, and make way for new ideas and fresh perspectives.

Three Steps to Behavioral Balance

1. **Get organized**: Improve your skills in organization and time management. If you find it's impossible, ask yourself if you simply have too much on your plate, and then look at your life priorities.

2. **Put your health first**: Take note of your sleep patterns—are they replenishing you? Be aware of "self-medication" techniques—for example, look honestly at the amount of alcohol you drink and the times that you do. Are there any other addictive behaviors that may be supplying a quick fix to the emotional pain of stress?

3. **Incorporate wholesome activities into your life**: To combat stress, you need relaxation and pleasure, not more stress on your body through unhealthy habits, such as smoking, drinking, or overeating. Instead of going to the bar after work, unwind by taking your dog for a walk in the park, playing with your children, visiting a museum, or taking a yoga or Tai Chi class.

#5—Spiritual Balance

People often assume that "spiritual balance" in life means being part of organized religion. It can be, but not necessarily so. Larry S. Chapman, in the *American Journal of Health Promotion* (1987), defined spirituality as "the ability to discover and express your purpose in life; to learn how to experience love, joy, peace and fulfillment; and to help yourself and others achieve their full potential."

Doing this begins with developing self-awareness, which is the ability to discover and nurture who you are on the inside, regardless of the hustle and bustle of everyday life. You can begin by asking yourself, "Who am I and what do I stand for?" Ekhart Tolle, in *A New Earth: Awakening to Your Life's Purpose,* recounts the story of a schoolteacher in her mid-forties who had been given only a short time to live. It was not until this point in her life that she was able to find the "stillness" within that she never knew existed in her busy life as a schoolteacher. He tells us, "You are never more essentially, more deeply yourself than when you are still." Incorporating precious moments from our hectic lifestyles to experience our stillness on a daily basis is a necessity today for long-term health and inner peace.

When we have found our own stillness, we are then able to move beyond ourselves and connect with others in a serving capacity. Ralph Waldo Emerson wrote, "It is one of the most beautiful compensations of this life that no man can sincerely try to help another without helping himself." Providing service for others, volunteering our time, not only allows us to meet new people and share our skills and talents, but it allows us to effect change, have a positive impact on our communities, and gain a sense of achievement through championing a cause. It is a chance to give something back. If you take a moment to examine your life, you can probably see that you are already reaching out in your homes, in your communities, and in the lives of others. It is important that you acknowledge the incredible service you are doing, the impact you are having on those around you, and the spiritual dimension you are adding to your own life through this service.

Three Steps to Achieving Spiritual Balance

1. Change your life through self-awareness: It is through self-awareness that you identify and change the underlying core beliefs that drive destructive behaviors or create happiness. Start by analyzing your interests and skills, your strengths and weaknesses, your fears and dreams, your needs and values. Identify the qualities you value in others, and list the qualities that your friends would value in you. When you have begun to develop self-awareness, explore answers to the following deeper questions: Who am I? Why am I here? What is my purpose in life? How can I help others to fulfill their destiny?

2. Find your "stillness": You may find your stillness when you are enjoying nature, during meditation in quiet morning hours in your home, while reading religious texts or other spiritual material, and during those times when your mind is free of outside burdens and cares.

3. Examine your life: List those ways in which you are currently serving others in your home, your community, and your work. Celebrate the difference you are making in the lives of others. If you find this an area where you are lacking, look for opportunities to provide service to those in need, either on your own or through programs in your community.

Putting It All Into Action

We've looked at the five-part approach to greater life balance. Now it is time to put this new knowledge and approach into an action plan. The Stress Management Plan exercise below will help you create a powerful visual picture of managing stress optimally. Commit to following through with your plan and build accountability and rewards into it. Write down your goals and keep them displayed where you can view them several times a day. Share your goals with a friend or family member who will support and encourage you in your endeavor. And be willing to sacrifice your old ways to achieve a new way of thinking, reacting, and living. The benefits will be well worth the effort!

My Stress Management Plan

Identify my life stressors. Thoughtfully identify what is causing the stress in your life (work, home, personal). Be as specific as possible:

_____
_____
_____

How is stress impacting me? Identify your body's physiological response to stress:

_____
_____
_____

How am I coping currently? What physical, intellectual, emotional, behavioral, or spiritual strategies do I presently utilize?

_____
_____
_____

Steps I Can Take to Achieve:

Intellectual/Cognitive Balance

_____
_____
_____
_____

Physical Balance

_____
_____
_____
_____

Emotional Balance

_____
_____
_____
_____

Behavioral Balance

_____
_____
_____
_____

Spiritual Balance

_____
_____
_____
_____

It's no secret that we live in an increasingly stressful environment. Our own wellness is the key to being effective in our homes, our families, and our workplaces; and acknowledging, understanding, and dealing with our stress is essential to this. We need to utilize the positive stress in our lives to enhance our personal growth and spur us on to greater achievements. Through informed choices, we can learn to counteract the negative effects of stress. By achieving balance in five key areas—intellectual, physical, emotional, behavioral, and spiritual—we can gain a renewed sense of happiness and well-being, and an energy that comes from living a stress-enhanced rather than stress-depleted lifestyle.

Joanne Steed-Takasaki

Joanne Steed-Takasaki is a stress management consultant and motivational speaker, and the owner of JOSTA Consulting, Inc. She has had the opportunity of presenting extensively in both business and educational settings, and has worked with such clients as the Mirage Hotel and Casino and the Monte Carlo Hotel and Casino in Las Vegas. Joanne has a passion for health and wellness, and a mission to help others achieve knowledge, balance and success in their lives.

Joanne has her master's degree in education, and associate diplomas from Trinity College in London (England), Mount Royal College in Calgary, and the Conservatory at the University of Toronto. She has a love of learning, and is continually engaged in new courses and seminars.

A teacher for 25 years, Joanne is also a certified Fitness Consultant and Personal Fitness Trainer. The loves of her life are her husband, Bob, her children, Christopher, Jayme and Brad, and her two Yorkshire terriers, Gizmo and Tobi. Her passions are spending time with her family, traveling, reading, weight training, circuit training, and helping others achieve their potential.

Business Name: JOSTA Consulting, Inc.,
Address: 2124 17 Avenue, Coaldale, AB T1M 1K1
Telephone: 403-330-6703
Email: joanne@jostaconsulting.com
Web Address: www.jostaconsulting.com

Favorite Quote:

In everyone's life, at some time, our inner fire goes out. It is then burst into flame by an encounter with another human being. We should be thankful for those people who rekindle the inner spirit.

Albert Schweitzer

Margaret Barrie

InspiraConsulting

Success in the Multi-Generational Workplace

In the workplace, we are many, we are different, and we have differing points of views and expectations. The real question is, are we productive and are we getting the best out of our people. Do we need to do something different? Do we need to rethink our leadership strategy? What we are looking for today is an ageless, homogenous, harmonious, mind-melding workplace. Is it realistic? Is it right? We really must learn to accept the diversity in our workplaces—especially those related to age. With guidelines and strategies in place, and lots of coaching on the part of our current leaders, we can create a successful, productive, multi-generational workforce. The first and most important step in any strategy is identifying the target, knowing that where you need to go and how you get there will follow. Another very important point to consider is who are the players?

Walking into any business setting these days is a lesson in generational blending. We may see as many as four generations. We have **Traditionalists,** born before the end of World War II (1925–1942), often referred to as the *Silent Generation*. Most of this generation are long past retirement age, but have chosen to continue to work, or have come back to work, perhaps because of financial need or maybe because they are bored. Whatever the reason, we need them. They have a lot of expertise from which we need to learn. It is critical to the success of any business for the traditionalists to share their intellectual capital with their team members.

Then, of course, we have the **Baby Boomers**, the generation to which I proudly belong, born from 1943–1960 (and I will admit to no more than that). The Baby Boomers have been part of many very significant political and cultural events. For the most part, Baby Boomers still occupy the senior-level management offices. This age group still effects change and wields a great deal of power. Baby Boomers give new meaning to growing old, now that "50 is the new 30"—a philosophy to which I sincerely subscribe.

To move on to the younger generations, we would need to start with **Generation X.** The members of this group were born between 1961 and 1981, and they are sometimes referred to as *Baby Busters* and the *13th Generation*. The Baby Busters were raised by the Baby Boomers, and are often considered self-indulgent, mobile, and materialistic. They have been taught to be self-reliant and independent, as many have come from a single-parent family or a two-income household. They have been raised with gender, racial, and ethnic diversity.

Moving along to the **Y Generation**, this group was born between 1982 and 2002. They have been called many different names: Millennial, Net Generation, the Digital Generation, or **Gen-Me**. They know more about computers and comparable technology than any other generation so far. These people live and breathe technology and are beginning to move into the workplace in large numbers. We need to understand who they are and how to work with and lead them optimally.

Strengths and Weaknesses

Every generation comes with its own strengths and weaknesses. As a leader and co-worker, it is helpful to be aware of what these are. Know that strengths and weaknesses are often in the eyes of the beholder. What a Traditionalist may see as a weakness, a Boomer may see as a strength.

Traditionalists have practical experience and knowledge of what worked and did not work in the past. This is valuable information, very necessary for making critical organizational changes. They have a lot of expertise that can only be shared from person to person. This kind of knowledge is not written anywhere and is only learned through experience. This kind of knowledge is priceless during the organizational planning and running of any business.

Awakening the Workplace

Traditionalists are, by nature, culturally loyal and optimistic in the workforce. Good support to have on the side of the business! They are hard workers and like to be recognized for their work. As a leader, you can rely on the traditionalist as a pillar for the business to lean on through good times or bad. Their optimism can be invaluable to leaders at times when support for decisions is necessary to implement changes to bring more growth or productivity to the business.

Their strengths do not necessarily lie in the communication-technology side of the business and they may need a little extra support in that area. Their views of work–life balance may be different from those of the younger generations. They are from the years of being "loyal to the end" and sticking with one company until you retire. This is not the current way people view work–life balance, and this may cause differences of opinion with the younger generations. As a leader, it will be important to watch for underlying discontentment because of differing value systems.

Boomers were the first to feel the need for self-fulfillment, personally and professionally. They were bound to set new norms with their traditionalist parents. They focused on self-growth and unfulfilled potentials. Boomers are particularly adept at team building and developing leadership within the team. They enjoy working and learning in teams, so they lean toward group discussions, consensual decision making, and fairness in the workplace. These are very strong values that, as a leader, you should capitalize on frequently. Knowing you have this kind of workplace asset, you should be able to make smooth, speedy, effective changes to accommodate the needs of your business. You should be able to find support for most everything you need to do.

Boomers do have a need to be personally gratified, sometimes more than what the job can support or the project will allow. A little like a needy friend, they can become a bit overwhelming. Leaders will need to watch for signs of this and catch any problems that may result because of it. You may be confronted with a disgruntled employee if he or she is not carefully handled. It is much harder to turn them around than it is to stop this from happening in the first place.

Gen-Xers inherited the workforce from Boomers. This brought a big change in the culture, as Gen-Xers wanted work–life balance. They wanted to be able to enjoy life and family, which was unheard of with the Boomers. As a result, they brought technology, such as laptops, into the workplace to build in mobility and flexibility, saving hundreds of thousands of dollars for companies everywhere. Even though there were some tensions in the beginning, since it looked as though they didn't have the same work ethic as the Boomers, the work still got done and businesses were still successful. Managers and leaders needed to loosen up their management style and learn to trust their people to manage their own time and projects. Gen-Xers are self-reliant and well-balanced people. They don't require a lot of supervision and, in fact, probably work better without it. They do have a need for leadership feedback—a kind of "How am I doing today?" check. They respond well to praise. They work hard and more diligently because of it.

The Gen-Xers can often be accused of being self-focused and somewhat disloyal to the business. This may be a direct result of some of their parents' experiences in their own careers. This is a difficult issue for leaders to deal with, but keeping an open dialogue with all employees is critical for successful employee retention. Knowing them will help to understand what makes them tick—what they need to feel fulfilled.

Gen-Me's have a natural instinct to move through the world as self-reliant, important members of society. They are globally aware and concerned. Their knowledge of technology is a great asset to any business and they will provide the kind of workforce a leader needs to keep on the leading edge of success. Leaders of Gen-Me's are charged with keeping them as updated as possible with cybercommunication. If they feel as though they are falling behind, they will move on. They are driven to make their work meaningful. The confidence and positive self-esteem of Gen Me's gives managers the kind of team members who can accomplish almost any project and pull together when needed.

Gen-Me's work to live; therefore, they demand work–life balance. They value regular hours and time off. A Baby Boomer or Traditionalist leader may find it somewhat difficult to accept personal life coming first. The secret is to find the acceptable balance. Since time off is the currency, remember to use it as a reward for extra effort, if possible. Finding the time is not always possible, but being flexible is.

Gen-Me's also don't care for close supervision and hands-on management.

Awakening the Workplace

Managing from a distance and allowing them to make some of their own decisions is important, since this is the way of most Gen-Me's. This will lead them to confidence and personal success. More about this later on.

Leading the Masses

So, how do we bring this all together? What is our focus? Where do we go from here? I think the questions we really need to ask are, "What do we, as leaders, expect from them?" and "What do we realistically think we can get from so many different styles in our teams?"

#1—Success

Gen-Me's look for and need instant gratification, and they expect to be successful immediately. It is the employer's task to convince them that it won't happen that fast in the real world. They will need to work for it and "put in their time." The good news is that they like to work hard and are willing to do so but will expect high praise and plenty of it. Gone are the days of thinking, "If I quietly work hard someone will notice me." Today's attitude is notice me now and notice me a lot or I'll go somewhere else where they do notice me. Gen-Xers are much the same, so a steady diet of rewarding feedback will go a long way toward the successful completion of projects and a harmonious working environment.

#2—Performance

Annual performance evaluation used to be the standard and it was fine for the Baby Boomers, and to some extent the Gen-Xers, because that method was handed down to us from our predecessors. This method now needs to be updated or eliminated. Leadership needs to update performance constantly and manage by being present. This does not mean micromanaging, but rather that leaders be visible and present in a way that allows their team to know they are there and accessible. "Hands-on" leadership is a more accurate name for it. You are part of the team—a go-to person. The big glass office should be done away with. The separation is too great, the manager too inaccessible. The mindset today has less to do with chain of command and more to do with equality. The larger the gap between you and your team, the less you will know about them. In order to coach them well, you need to know and understand their strengths and weaknesses. Be aware of the people who tend to monopolize your time. Be fair with your time and try to give it to everyone equally.

#3—Boundaries and Limits

Once you have your teams and your projects identified, the coaching begins. Identify your team norms. How does the team work together? What are the expectations of the team in terms of behavior? For example, simple etiquette may dictate no calls after 9 p.m. or before 8 a.m. What one generation considers a socially acceptable behavior may not be okay with another generation. A 21-year-old project manager calling a 55-year-old customer Sally or George rather than Ms. or Mr. might not work very well, whereas this would be more acceptable if the project manager were 55 years old as well and had 30 years of experience under his or her belt. This all goes back to knowing your team and getting the correct fit. Leaders set the targets, the numbers, the goals for the business, and the people, and then they match the talent to those targets based on their knowledge of the team. This is critical to success. This is not something you can take chances with; you must be good at it. Moving people around in the middle of a project is costly in terms of money and self-confidence. Matching people is costly if you get it wrong. So, it is critical to know your team from the beginning. Learn what your team can do and how far they can stretch. Then congratulate them for it when they succeed.

#4—Motivation

Think baby steps, because small praises can turn into big wins. It's human nature to want approval from people we respect, regardless of our generation. Small praises like "good work," "good idea," or "sounds like you know what you're doing" all motivate people to want to hear it again. Pride promotes more pride; success brings on more success. Being conscientious is considered the single most important trait any employee can have. It is even considered more important than intelligence.

Some people don't even recognize these traits in themselves. It is the job of the manager to recognize and develop them. A conscientious employee will have good attendance records, high productivity, and be generally cooperative and creative. These are key traits to look for in your people. Watch for it and develop it to its full potential. If we can look past the generational differences in attitude, style of dress, and lifestyle, we have the makings of successful, effective employees. It is our job to discover their attributes and develop them.

It is important to present an open, clear, and approachable manner. The leaders of today are really the connective tissue of the team. Motivating your team means getting to know them as people, as well as generations.

Nothing really changes when dealing with the human ego and sensitivities. No matter what generation you come from, we all respond to clear direction.

#5—Hiring

As leaders, we are charged with bringing the best out of all the employees, no matter what their backgrounds. This begins by hiring the correct people for the job or the project. Being part of the hiring process is very important to the success of a project and to your success. Be careful to select the correct people for your office environment, for your project, and for your style of leadership. It is very important to not just hire for the project. Employee selection should not be an isolated decision. Get some help with this from someone else on your team, someone you trust who knows what fits into your team environment.

The B.B.C. Approach to Teams

To construct and lead a generationally diverse team, I have found the B.B.C. approach to be a very successful method. The three prongs to this approach are **B**uild, **B**lend, and **C**oach. The following are the three key elements of this model and some strategies to make them work:

Build

It is critical that you know what kind of team you want to build. Does your team need to work together in partnership? Do they need to work independently but come back to the team when their part of the project is completed? In both of these scenarios, the leader needs to understand what kind of person it takes to work on each of these types of teams. You need to understand the challenges each team member will face on their particular team.

What are the tools they will need to do their jobs? It will be your job to outfit them as you would if they were climbing Mount Everest. They need tools, training, and guidance. None of this can be done if you don't clearly understand the project, the team, and the potential team members.

Understanding the strengths you will need to form your team will be very important. Perhaps you need to have someone who is a mathematical wizard; someone who is practically experienced in a particular technology; or someone who has grown up with the technology. These are just examples of ways to think through choosing people for your team. How will they gel with the rest of the team? Can they work with the group? This is a very important part of any hiring decision to ensure good business results.

How do you know you have the right fit? That comes from knowing your people. Get to know who they are. What are their strengths and weakness? What is it that makes them work harder? What makes them bond together and get the job done in a crunch? Which team member will work the extra hours to get an important project across the finish line without grumbling about it, or expecting something special for it? Who steps up to the plate when needed?

Blend

How well do their personalities and working styles fit with other members of the team? They may not be similar, but may be complementary. I once had a diversified team in terms of age difference and work style. At one time, I had an older female employee with a lot of experience on the practical side of the business. She had seen nearly every scenario possible. She didn't have a lot of experience in new technology, however, and struggled with trying to learn and keep up with every new revision. I also had a young man, lacking in practical experience but exuding so much confidence that it came across as arrogance. However, his technical skills were amazing. As a team, they got the job done, although not without some scars. The woman employee always walked away feeling intimidated; the man felt she treated him like a child. After a lot of individual discussions and continued assignments, they came to understand each other better and recognized that they could use each other's strengths to their own benefit. The young man needed her practical experience as a guide for building his own. She was there for him, which provided credibility with the customer. She could give him the guidance he needed when a tough decision had to be made. He helped her gain her confidence with the new technology. With each new revision of the software, she picked it up faster and with more confidence. She stopped being intimidated, and he felt she no longer treated him like a child but as an equal. It was also important for me to know them well enough to be sure they would work it out without my intervention. I bolstered her confidence and made suggestions to him about backing off a little.

Understanding what your people are good at goes a long way toward building a successful team. Often people are good at several things and are interested in developing more than one skill, especially the Gen-Me's. This is a much-sought-after benefit, for both the employee and employer. Team building, of course, includes building the skills of individual employees. Employees see skill development as receiving recognition from the organization and as the organization offering a chance for personal growth. Cross-training also builds flexibility into an organization.

Coach

As leaders of all the different generations, it is up to us to find out what it is that team members need to work efficiently and productively. Really, as a leader, we are a coach, a facilitator, and a mentor. Implementing mentoring programs so that older, more experienced employees can mentor the younger generations also spreads the coaching job around. This ensures that Traditionalists and Baby Boomers have an opportunity to pass on their experience and knowledge. It also gives them an incentive to continue to work and a valuable position on the team and in the business. It sets a good example for the rest of the team to work hard and be dedicated. It promotes long tenures for employees. It promotes the commitment your business needs to be successful. It is also a model for the behavior you want to encourage from the Gen-Xers and Gen-Me's, or any generation for that matter.

The key is to know your people better than you have ever needed to know them before. You also need to get to know them faster than you have before. It is critical to understand what makes them tick—what is important to them. Praise and feedback are necessary on an ongoing basis, not once a year. Feedback will not always be good, but it is important to provide it in an atmosphere that reassures the employee that the purpose is growth, not criticism. Lead close up; it will pay off in the long run.

Every generation needs coaching and every generation likes feedback. Be careful to make sure you treat everyone the same. If you coach the Gen-Me's, make sure you also coach the Baby Boomers. If you give praise and feedback to the Gen-Xers, give praise and feedback also to the Traditionalists. Never leave anyone out. They may not need as much coaching, but they will always need praise and feedback.

The leader is the link between the business and the employee. Employees get their signals from you. If you are positive and upbeat, they will feel positive and upbeat too.

The Future for Generations to Come

The Gen-Xers and Gen-Me's are our next generation of business leaders, teachers, inventors, and politicians. In short, they will be the ones in charge. Earlier in the chapter, I mentioned that Gen-Xers and Gen-Me's are not interested in leadership. That does seem to be the status now. However, it is simple human nature for people to step up to the plate when the call comes. What Baby Boomers and Traditionalists need to do is help to prepare them for it, as best we can.

We have choices in how to handle the generational combination. Learn who they are. Care about them more than you care about the project. Learn to be the best listener possible. Be a good coach and mentor. Show your team what it is like to be ethical and generous. It will all come back to you a hundredfold.

Margaret Barrie

Margaret Barrie is an accomplished international speaker and marketing consultant with over 25 years of speaking experience on a wide range of topics. Her expertise, which she shares with corporations, associations and community organizations, includes carefully crafted presentations and keynotes on corporate leadership, facilitation, mentoring, communication and team building.

Margaret's messages of how to build and lead teams are memorable and powerful, and she has created and inspired many teams to success. Through building their self-esteem and confidence and by giving them the tools they need to become leaders, Margaret inspires people to be all they can be.

Her education has included courses at Crotonville Business Academy, NY, the University of California at Los Angeles, and Madison University in Mississippi. Her credentials include a Bachelor of Science degree in psychology.

Margaret sits on the board of directors for the Ernestine's Women's Shelter. She is a member of Toastmasters International and sits on the executive of one of the local chapters. Margaret is also a member of the United Way Speakers Bureau.

Business Name:	InspiraConsulting
Address:	550 Farmstead Drive, Milton, ON L9T 4M3
Telephone:	905-864-9298
Email:	m.barrie@sympatico.ca
Speaking Affiliations:	Canadian Association of Professional Speakers, Toastmasters International

The real voyage of discovery consists not in seeking new landscapes, but in having new eyes.

Marcel Proust

Louise Diotte, CFP, EPC

Associated with Investors Group Financial Services Inc.

Living Your Best Life Journey

After 25 years in the financial industry, it is clear to me that *money does not buy happiness; however, living your best life journey does*. Your best life journey can be defined as realizing all your hopes and dreams, being proud of your accomplishments, and being proud especially of the profound legacy that you leave behind for others to carry on. You need to take the time to purposefully explore what your best life journey means to you and to explore how your personal vision is connected to financial planning.

As individuals, and especially as women, we need to feel empowered by our natural financial skills. We need to listen to our inner common sense when it comes to money matters. We need to look deep inside our soul to embrace and develop our personal vision and to incorporate this personal vision within our financial plan. I can tell you from experience with my own clients that the more we believe in realizing our best life journey, the easier it is to achieve financial freedom.

The Wisdom of Children

As children, we are born with two of the greatest gifts: 1) life, and 2) the ability to make a difference in our world. During our formative years, all of us develop a sense of what this difference could be. We have all heard the following from children: "When I grow up I will become a fireman" (or a teacher, a doctor, a veterinarian, a social worker, a nurse, a dentist, a hairstylist…). These answers often can be related to whatever Mom's or Dad's profession is. Children tend to look at their surroundings and want to emulate the people that change their world.

The notion of living our best life journey starts with the person whom we see as our hero. At this stage in our young lives, it is not about the money, it is about who makes us feel important, who cares for us, who smiles at us, who makes us laugh, who protects us and who stands up for us. As children, we already know what is important in our lives. As adults, we need to tap into what we already knew back then by asking ourselves important key questions, which we will look at later in this chapter.

How do adults lose touch with this basic knowledge that they already had as children? Life evolves at lightning speed, especially during teenage years when there are more conflicting thoughts that come in to shake that notion of living out a best life journey. Outside influences throughout your life will want to pull you away from living your best life journey. The day-to-day minutiae take over and you tend to go with the flow of life, letting this flow dictate who you are.

You graduate, start a career, get married and start a family. As you attain these goals and dreams, you acquire things: an apartment or house, furnishings, a car—just to name a few. Along with these things come the student loans, the rent and/or mortgage, the car loan and the credit cards. The prevalence of easy credit today makes it easy to live outside your means. The "buy now, pay later" syndrome makes it really easy to lose control over your financial destiny. Let me cite an example: Thirty years ago, a "monthly payment" would have referred to a car loan or a mortgage. Credits cards were almost non-existent and personal loans were very hard to obtain. Our parents had no choice but to save up for purchases. Today, you can get credit everywhere you shop, you can obtain loan approval on-line, and you can transfer balances from one credit card to another. As long as you make your monthly payments on time, you will continue to receive more credit. If this "buy now, pay later" syndrome makes life seems so easy, then why are so many people stressed about financial matters?

The answer to this question lies in taking back the control of your life destiny by controlling your financial destiny. You have to sit and look at your financial picture, however hard it may seem, and become aware of what you actually pay out in interest to these credit card companies. It is an exercise that most people find very difficult; this is why it is important to go back to basics by asking the following three important questions:

1. What do you really want out of life?
2. What will make you happy?
3. What would you like to be remembered for?

Examining the answers to these questions can open up a great discussion which can lead you to describe what your best life journey would look like if you had control over it. You create your own personal vision which acts as a guiding light through this financial maze. Once this personal vision light is guiding you, you will find it easier to look at your financial picture and you will be able to start making changes and choices that will bring you back into control of your life and finances. If you have a clear sense of what your goal is, you are better prepared to make the choices and changes that will lead you on a successful journey.

At this point, you may say that you don't have credit card problems. (Your parents may have taught you to be afraid of them.) You are one step ahead. However, it is still very important to ask the same three questions to develop your best life journey in order for it to guide you towards the next level of success.

In answering these questions, you may find that you are already living your best life journey but that the day-to-day "busyness" of life had not allowed you to realize this fact. You will suddenly feel a sense of accomplishment and be proud of where you are.

Our Need to Dream

We need to dream and to create a personal vision of where we want our life journey to lead us. We need to find out what motivates us. We need to know what we are passionate about. We need to create our eulogy. We need to create in our minds the person we want to become in the eyes of our family, our workplace and our community, and we also need to know who we would like to become for ourselves. What would make us proud, and more importantly, happy? Once we have painted this picture of what we would like our lives to be, it is then possible to start seeing our future just as you would see a well-thought-out vacation plan.

Your dreams and your personal vision will guide you to make the right choices in your life and in your financial life in order for you to live your best life journey. This does not mean that you won't encounter unforeseen stops in your best life journey. Just as you do when you go on vacation, you will definitely run into some good unforeseen events and maybe some bad unforeseen events in your life and financial life. These moments will make a profound impact on your life journey; without a doubt, however, you will be better prepared to accept the challenges if you have taken the time to map out a plan.

When you have good life surprises, you can usually glide through them. However, it is often the bad unforeseen circumstances from which you learn your best life lessons. I believe that the reason we must face challenges in our lives and financial lives is to learn life lessons. We can be better prepared to face these challenges if we have our personal vision with us.

**Once you are armed with your personal life vision
and you are ready to live your best life journey every
single day of your life, you then start seeing the
financial picture more clearly than ever before.**

Help Is on the Way!

In this fast-paced world, we cannot know it all ourselves. We need the specific knowledge of others. To align your "best life journey" with your financial vision, a financial consultant is a necessary asset. Here are a few things to consider as you are seeking a financial consultant:

Getting back on the right path: You may sense that you are not living your best life journey, that somewhere along the road you made a financial choice that was not the best. You can still rethink your plan and restate your personal vision. Seek professional financial help from an individual who will guide you back onto your right path. This situation often happens; we are so busy in trying to identify ourselves that we forget some pieces along the way. The thing to remember in this case is simply that we have the power to change our life path at any time in our lives. It is never too late to take a different route. We have to remember that our life is much more versatile than a Monopoly game. This is one of the true beauties in life. We can continually reinvent ourselves if we allow it to happen.

Time to plan: Until now you may not have put much thought into mapping out your personal life vision and/or how you would live your best life journey. You have the power to change your life at any point in time. You need to map out your life the same way you would a vacation.

Few people leave for a vacation without having pre-booked their flight, their hotel rooms and their rental cars. Some even know every stop they will make during this vacation, including the amount of time they will spend on the beach. This does not mean that once they get to their destination and discover new opportunities or encounter unforeseen challenges they do not change their plans. The same amount of careful, thorough planning time should apply to our personal life vision and life journey.

Dare to dream: The dilemma we face in planning out our best life journey is quite simply that it is not as tangible as a vacation, or as tangible as buying a house or acquiring a new car. As a financial consultant, I see my competition not as other financial consultants or other financial institutions but as the consumer world. For instance, most of us like the feel of a new car, the look, the drive, even the smell of a new car. This makes it so easy to accept that high financial commitment of monthly car payments that usually range between $250 and $800. However, we cannot feel our future, we cannot smell our future, and we can only dream about our future; therefore, it is easier to accept the $500 monthly car payment than the $500 monthly retirement savings plan contribution. Often we are told as children to stop daydreaming, to live in reality. So, unfortunately, we don't dare to dream. We say, "Dreams won't pay the bills." Well, I say, "Dare to dream," for it is these dreams that will entice you to make the necessary financial changes to follow your best life journey.

Take action: Once you are back on the right path, by taking a serious look and allowing yourself to dream, you should have a clear vision of your best life journey. You now need to convey this vision to a financial professional who will help you take the vision to the level you deserve by applying good financial strategies that will lift the financial stress you often feel and ensure that you remain in control at all times. I like to describe the latter as *making your money work harder than you do without adding additional, undue risk*.

Who Should You Consult?

Financial Planners Standards Council (FPSC) is a member of Financial Planning Standards Board Ltd. FPSB was established in October 2004 by 17 non-profit associations that together will certify over 45,000 individuals outside the U.S. to use the CFP, CERTIFIED FINANCIAL PLANNER and ![CFP] marks and that will join FPSB as members. FPSB will protect financial planning consumers and foster professionalism in financial planning through the ongoing development and enforcement of relevant international competency and ethics standards. CFP professionals can be found in every segment of the Canadian financial services industry, helping clients to meet their personal goals. Education, examination, experience, and ethics are all part of becoming a CFP. It is a high standard that you should be demanding of your financial planner since you are entrusting them with your financial affairs.

Choosing a Financial Planner

Don't let an advisor define who you are by looking at the money you have; instead, let them define you by your life goals and your personal vision. Look for the professional who understands how to apply the Six-Step Financial Planning Process to your specific best life journey plan to generate the right financial plan for you. Your goal should be to find a competent, qualified professional with whom you feel comfortable and whose business style suits your financial planning needs.

The six disciplines of financial planning are as follows:[2]

1. *To establish, discuss and agree on a client/planner engagement which should explain the issues and concepts related to your overall financial plan. This*

---

1   ![CFP] ™ Certified Financial Planner™ and CFP™ are certification marks awarded by Financial Planners Standards Council under a license agreement with Financial Planning Standards Board Ltd. (FPSB).

2. The six disciplines of financial planning were taken from the Financial Planners Standards Council website.

engagement should also explain the services he or she will provide and the process of planning and documentation. It should also clarify your responsibilities as a client and clarify his or her responsibilities as your planner. This engagement should also include a discussion about how and by whom he or she will be compensated.

2. *Your planner should be ready to help you gather the necessary financial data, and obtain information about your financial resources and obligations through interviews or questionnaires. Your planner should be well aware of your financial data and your personal vision before giving you the advice you need to fulfill your goals. A planner should be in a position to help you map out your best life journey, your needs and priorities. Investigate your values, preferences, financial outlook and desired results as they relate to your best life journey and personal vision.*

3. *Your planner should also be able to clarify your present financial status and identify any problem areas and opportunities.*

4. *Your planner should develop and present a financial plan tailored to meet your best life journey, your personal vision, your values, your temperament and your risk tolerance while providing projections and recommendations. Establish an appropriate review cycle.*

5. *Your planner should assist you in implementing the recommendations discussed if you so wish. This may involve coordinating contacts with other professionals such as accountants and lawyers, with your permission.*

6. *Finally, your plan should be monitored to ensure that both you and your planner keep on track and are prepared to weather any circumstances that may arise.*

This process may seem overwhelming to some of you; however, a qualified professional should be able to simplify the process for you greatly. The emphasis here is the importance of choosing the right individual who would follow the Six-Step Financial Planning Process. Financial consultants deal with your hard-earned money. Your entire financial future is at stake; therefore, you need to choose wisely.

For more information on the CFP designation, please visit the Financial Planning Standards Council website at www.cfp-ca.org

Women's Wisdom

Women need to realize their capabilities as good money managers. For years, women have been programmed to think that the financial world is a man's world; however, we have daily examples of great women excelling in business and in the financial world. Women truly have an inner common sense that is necessary for a successful financial future. This inner common sense comes mainly from the need to protect our loved ones. We are usually not huge risk takers; most women want to know that their money is keeping pace with inflation and is not at risk. Actually, we have definitely started to see a shift during the past 10 years: there are more women willing to take the financial world by storm and there are also more men willing to take on less risk in their lives.

Good, strong communication between life partners about financial matters concerning their combined best life journey is definitely a must for a long-lasting relationship. Don't be afraid to talk about money. For years, people did not talk about money matters in a family setting. The running joke in our industry is that people would prefer to talk about sex in a family setting than money matters... We need to talk openly about money matters, with our partner and with our children.

It is vitally important as parents to talk to our children (both girls and boys) about their financial future. The reason for this is that we live in a very different world than our ancestors did a mere 100 years ago. For example, when my grandfather was born in 1901, his life expectancy was 50 to 60 years. Today, babies are born with a life expectancy of at least 80 to 85 years. This number increases with each year that we live; therefore, our children will have to ensure that their financial future is secured for a much longer time than our grandparents, our parents and even we have had to. Our children will see more people living to the age of 115 to 120 (hard to believe but true). With technological and medical advancements and with better living conditions, we are extending our lifespan in a good way; therefore, we need to also extend our financial life in the same way. Just think that if we talk to our children today, in simplified terms, about financial matters, about their own best life journey, we may keep them from repeating some of the mistakes that we may have made along the way.

With the parents' approval, I often visit with the children of my clients to discuss how they feel about financial matters. Their enthusiasm and candid responses always pleasantly surprise me. As professionals, we can simplify the process for them to understand in their own terms. The following are a few of the topics and strategies that I often discuss with them.

Tips for Talking With Your Children About Money

1. Pay yourself first to ensure your financial freedom. Take your earnings from the first hour of each day and invest them to ensure financial freedom. I often bring this tip to the attention of teenagers; it is easier for them to see this possibility since, other than, say, the Olsen twins, they usually don't earn high hourly wages yet. As a result, they absorb this investment concept more rapidly, and once the habit has formed, it is simpler for them to continue doing the same in later years.

2. Beware of credit cards. I explain to them how credit cards work and that maxing out on credit cards leads to making monthly payments for a very long time. They learn that typical interest rates charged on credit cards range from 18 to 28 percent, and that, therefore, what may have appeared to have been bought on sale using a credit card will end up costing more in the long run. I emphasize the darker side of not making their payments on time. Most credit card companies are tied electronically to credit bureau reports, and if payments are not made by the due date, a bad mark goes against their credit status. A bad credit bureau report (hence a bad report card) will hurt them the most when they will need to borrow for the purchase of a home or to finance their own business. There are even some credit card companies that will now automatically increase the interest rate charged on the account (for example, if you are currently paying 17.9 percent per annum and forget to make a few payments by the due date, the credit card company will increase the interest rate charged to 24 percent).

If driven properly, however, a credit card can also be a valuable financial vehicle. It alleviates our need to carry large sums of cash at any one time and it allows us to confirm reservations when we travel. A parent would not hand over the car keys to a child without properly teaching him or her how to drive the vehicle; therefore, why would a parent give a credit card to a young adult without first providing proper instructions?

3. Be tax savvy. We often hear, "If I earn too much money, it all goes away in taxes, so why bother earning more money?" This statement is *fortunately* wrong. In Canada, we have a gradual tax system in which the marginal tax rate increases in percentage as you make more money, so that it would be easy for people to think that earning more money would lead to more taxes. Here are some points that I cover with teenagers to show the opposite:

- First, I ask them to describe what they aspire to be since it is more important to love your work than to love the money that you can derive from it. If you love your work, it is not a burden to do it. They will have a better sense of accomplishment which will form part of their best life journey. I usually get great responses which allow me to encourage them to continue to dream about their best life journey.

- Next, I explain to them how the earned income and the income taxes taken from this income work in Canada: Take, for instance, a starting base salary of $30,000 per year with the promise of salary increases over time. Well $30,000 in Canada would incur approximately $3,800 to $6,500 in income taxes, depending on which province or territory you live in, leaving $23,500 to $26,200 of disposable cash. If that base salary increases to $100,000, this amount would incur approximately $26,000 to $36,000 in taxes, leaving $64,000 to $74,000 of net income. This example shows them that earning more income does not mean you give it all up in taxes. And they can clearly see that a person can do more with $74,000 in net income than with $26,200.

4. Dream with a purpose. Once I have taught them this lesson about taxes, I remind them that money is not everything and that money does not buy happiness. The real lesson is that if they happen to be fortunate enough to earn enough net disposable income, they should spend responsibly, show appreciation and give back to their community, and ultimately live to fulfill their best life journey. I remind them to keep on dreaming with a purpose.

5. Live within your means. With children, we cover the "buy now and pay later" syndrome. They are forewarned how to control its temptation.

Over the years, I have had opportunities to work with many people to make sense of their financial affairs and through this I have discovered that people want to leave a lasting legacy of who they are and not of how much they earn or accumulate. People want to be known for who they are and not for the size of their wallets. Guiding my clients to live their best life journey by delivering sound, comprehensive financial advice for their family's peace of mind, today, tomorrow and beyond is my way of creating my lasting legacy. Empower yourself to create your own lasting legacy. May you be empowered to face your financial future with enthusiasm and may you live out your best life journey.

Louise Diotte, CFP, EPC

Louise Diotte is a financial planner who holds the CFP designation and the Elder Planner Counsellor designation. She guides and encourages her clients to live their best life journey. Louise's services include in-depth analysis to determine a client's best life journey, comprehensive financial planning, investor's risk profile analysis, as well as the following strategies: estate tax and business succession planning; charitable planned giving; tax planning; life, disability, critical illness and long-term care insurance strategies; retirement and investment strategy planning; and cash management.

Louise has over 29 years of experience in the financial industry, 15 of these spent as a corporate banker, and 14 as a financial consultant associated with Investors Group Financial Services. This broad knowledge has given Louise the tools she needs to help guide her clients through the financial maze, simplifying the process for them.

Business Name: Associated with Investors Group Financial Services Inc.
Address: 1730 St Laurent Blvd, Suite 430, Ottawa, ON K1G 5L1
Telephone: 613-742-8018 ext. 268; toll-free 1-888-713-3414
Email: louise.diotte@investorsgroup.com
Web Address: www.louisediotte.com
Professional Memberships: Financial Planning Standards Council, Canadian Initiative for Elder Planning Studies, Canadian Association of Gift Planners, Ottawa Estate Planning Council, Chambre de la Sécurité Financière du Québec

Favorite Saying:
Money doesn't buy happiness; however, living your best life journey does.

DeWayne Owens

Maximum Motivation Training Systems

Career Motivation: Finding PURPOSE in Your Work

For many years, I have been providing personal development and job readiness seminars for workforce centers and have seen the faces of literally thousands of men and women who have had to cope with the pressures, stress, and uncertainty involving unexpected unemployment. These people have become victims of company layoffs and downsizing. Yet, it is clear that there is another issue, especially for unemployed people between the ages of 35 and 50. They are facing the reality of being at a fork in the road of life and having to decide what to do with the rest of their lives and careers.

Of the vast number of people I have provided job readiness training to, only about 25 percent or less are actually involved in a career that they love and want to pursue. The other 75 percent are not excited about returning to the industry they have worked in for most of their lives. The only reason they are applying for jobs in their previous industry is that it's all they really know. It is the industry in which they have developed skills and knowledge and the one they have been paid to work in. Most of them were even considered to be "successful" in their career field, yet after all the years invested they have come out feeling unfulfilled and wanting a change. The problem is that they are not sure what it is they want to do next. They have a strong desire to do something other than what they were doing before, but the "new" or "something else" is the mystery that haunts them.

Whether you are employed or unemployed, you may find yourself experiencing the same feelings. You may have been in a career field that once brought you a feeling of significance; however, over the years you have lost your passion for the industry. You may very well feel that there is another career field or entrepreneurial opportunity to which you can give all of your passion and creative efforts. If this is the position you are in, know that you are absolutely right about your perceptions and assumptions. There *is* a career field available for you that will fuel your passion, enhance your talents, and where you will have a burning desire to excel. Yet, there is something essential for you to do to move forward with a new direction. In order to *discover* your dream career, you must understand your purpose or calling in life.

PURPOSE versus SUCCESS

Career success can be measured in a variety of ways. Some measure their success in terms of job satisfaction. Some measure it in terms of the salary they earn. Others measure their success in terms of their meaningful contribution to society or the clientele they serve. All of these factors and more are significant in measuring career success. You may have been successful, have contributed positively in more than one industry, and have been rewarded for your efforts. Your rewards may have come in the form of monetary compensation, awards, company recognition, such as "employee of the month," and so on. All of these rewards reflect a "measure" of success. You may have been told for most of your life that if you put your mind to it, you can achieve or become anything you desire. I most certainly agree that if you put enough time, effort, and work into something you can become successful at it. However:

What good does it do to climb the ladder of success only to find out that you've climbed up the wrong building?

Many people have worked all of their lives and have been successful in a career that never gave them the satisfying feeling they expected from it. In the almighty quest for success, relationships have been destroyed, families have been broken, and integrity has been compromised. Why? Because people have strived so hard to become successful that the cost they were willing to pay came above anything else, including relationships and their own integrity. Success and money have become the driving force behind their very existence. Although many have fallen prey to this vicious syndrome, many others have not gone down that path. Many people are good, decent, hard-working people who have simply dedicated their lives to a career that has now lost its luster.

The difference between success and purpose is the fact that you can be successful in many career venues without experiencing career satisfaction. When you are doing what you are purposed to do, that means you are doing what you were born to do. Doing what you are born to do means you are living out your calling in life. It means that you are doing what you absolutely love and are utilizing your God-given talents and abilities. When you are living your life *on purpose*, it means that you are doing what you are passionate about, and your creativity, innovation, and talents will take you to places you have never dreamed of. Knowing and engaging in your purpose will take you far above any success you could have ever experienced without realizing your life's calling.

**When your purpose meets divine opportunity, you will
know it without any doubt and you'll become unstoppable
in elevating yourself to the top of your profession.
When you begin making a living doing what you love to do,
you will never work another day in your life!**

ASSESSING your PURPOSE and PASSION

The most tragic thing that can happen to you is for you to live out your life without realizing what you were born to do. Until you are on your path of purpose, it does not matter how successful you may become in any career field, there will always be something on the inside of you eating away at your spirit. There will always be a void inside of you seeking fulfillment. You will look for something to fill the empty space in your heart that can only come by understanding and living out your God-given purpose in life.

This awesome purpose definitely extends into your career journey. Unfortunately, many people do not understand what their life's purpose is because they have allowed themselves to be caught up in the hectic hustle and bustle of life. We live in a fast-paced society that has lost its virtue for patience. This is particularly true of our careers. We have become a society so caught up in our jobs that we no longer take time out for ourselves. Instead of assessing our lives and careers, we just stick with what we know, because we do not have the time to process introspection. In order to discover what your purpose is in life, and how this purpose translates into a career, you **must** take time out to process pertinent questions regarding the rest of your life.

Purpose Direction Assessment

To assist you with this process, I've created an assessment tool I call the Purpose Direction Assessment. And, it is a tool with a mission! By completing it, you'll be placing yourself in the right direction for discovering and fulfilling your purpose in life. It will not uncover what your purpose ultimately is, but it will begin to give you clear insight about it. Now, embrace the idea that you were created with a purpose in mind. Completing the Purpose Direction Assessment exercise will give you a new perspective on your life and give you the motivation to make changes as well. Also, completing the Purpose Direction Assessment exercise will be an eye-opening experience for you. It may introduce you to a new you or confirm what you already know about yourself but have suppressed over the years. It can also provide a wake-up call for you.

In order to complete the Purpose Direction Assessment exercise, you will need to clear about an hour of uninterrupted time. Work on this exercise in a place where there will be very little distraction—preferably none. Although I want you to have fun with this exercise, it will at times require some concentrated thinking on your part, especially if you have no clue as to what your purpose is. Take your time and enjoy discovering or rediscovering yourself and your aspirations. Please allow yourself to have fun with the exercise and don't sweat the results. Remember, this is one hour that will impact your outlook on the rest of your life.

Finding M.E.A.N.I.N.G. in Your Life

You'll see below that the acronym M.E.A.N.I.N.G. represents the pillars of this assessment tool: motivation, empowerment, aspirations, natural abilities, inspiration, needs, and God. The first step is to answer each of these seven questions with seven answers, which you can put in the space below each one.

Motivation

What motivates you? What do you love to do? Think of such sources of motivation as people, stories, events, books, movies, learning, and so on.

1. _____   5. _____
2. _____   6. _____
3. _____   7. _____
4. _____

Empowerment

What are sources that empower you? When and how do you feel empowered?

1. _____   5. _____
2. _____   6. _____
3. _____   7. _____
4. _____

Aspirations

What do you aspire to do before you die? Think of variables that would add up to your dream lifestyle, for example, spending more time with family, changing career, growing closer to God, earning more money, living in a ideal location, traveling more, securing your family financially, and so on.

1. _____   5. _____
2. _____   6. _____
3. _____   7. _____
4. _____

Natural Abilities

What are things that you do naturally well? What are things that people have complimented you on? What are you good at?

1. _____   5. _____
2. _____   6. _____
3. _____   7. _____
4. _____

Inspiration

What inspires confidence in you? Think of sources of inspiration, such as people, stories, events, books, movies, learning, and so on.

1. _____   5. _____
2. _____   6. _____
3. _____   7. _____
4. _____

Needs

What is it that you need from life? What do you feel you must do before you die?

1. _____   5. _____
2. _____   6. _____
3. _____   7. _____
4. _____

God

How do you believe that spirituality plays a part in discovering your purpose? How important is God in your life?

1. _____   5. _____
2. _____   6. _____
3. _____   7. _____
4. _____

Now, choose the top three answers from each category and list them in order of priority. These top three answers from each question will give you laser-focused insight into what's truly important to you. Look carefully at your top three answers from each question. Look for similarities and connections in each category of answers. Begin to see how they relate, and intertwine your answers to formulate your purpose statement. Think of your answers as special ingredients to a recipe. After you have poured all of your special ingredients into a bowl and mixed them all up with a blender, what will they produce? Again, look your answers over carefully and formulate what they mean to you. Write down what you now think or perceive your life purpose to be:

_____

_____

_____

_____

Congratulations! You have now taken your first step toward fulfilling your purpose. You now have a greater awareness of your calling in life. There is no right or wrong way to answer your statement. It does not reflect right or wrong, it reflects what's inside of you. There is no mandatory word count. Your purpose statement is uniquely yours. At first, your purpose statement might seem a little awkward to you. You may look at it and say to yourself, "Now that I have my purpose statement written down, what am I supposed to do with it?"

» The first time I wrote out my purpose statement it simply read, "My purpose in life is to motivate and encourage people to be the best that they can be." Well, I did not know exactly what to do with my first purpose statement. At the time it was written, I had never given a speech before, much less considered being a motivational speaker. Nor, had I ever considered being an author. As time went on, my purpose in life began to unfold. As I listened to motivational speakers and preachers, it amazed me how awesome their impact was on the lives of other people. Their words were filled with hope, healing, encouragement, and empowerment. The most beautiful aspect of the messages of motivational speakers and preachers is that they are able to reach masses of people through their speeches, books, and recorded messages—whether on audiotape, CD, video, or DVD.

Before giving my first speech, I knew that a big part of my purpose would be fulfilled through motivational speaking and training. After that revelation, I joined Toastmasters International to learn how to give a speech, and the rest is history. **«**

As a result, I live out the purpose statement written many years ago, and now make a successful, fulfilling living by motivating and encouraging people to be the best that they can be. And I absolutely love it!

Moving Forward

Now that you have a purpose statement, be very choosy about who you share it with. Make sure that they are genuinely trustworthy and supportive. Know that even people who have good intentions have the potential to drain your hope through doubt. Life is challenging enough without inviting in more negativity. Believe me, there will come a time when you can boldly tell the whole world what your purpose is, no matter who may doubt you. But for now, follow my caution and be selective about sharing your Purpose Direction Assessment.

This exercise is only the beginning of the realization of your journey. It is an initial guide toward ultimately fulfilling your purpose. Update your Purpose Direction Assessment annually as you become more attuned to your purpose. You will find that your purpose statement may change slightly over time, but you will also notice that the underlying calling for your life will always remain the same. The awesome revelation of your purpose is that your eyes will be opened to how your purpose relates to a career path. You'll begin to believe in your purpose, develop your talents, and expand your creativity within your chosen industry. The final result, over time, will be the awesome blessing of making a living doing what you absolutely love to do. No person and no amount of money can ever take that joy away from you! Now, go forth and live your life **on purpose**!

DeWayne Owens

DeWayne Owens is the founder and president of Maximum Motivation Training Systems. He is a career enhancement specialist, bestselling author, trainer, consultant and nationally sought-after motivational speaker. DeWayne works with organizations that want to enhance peak performance, positivity, and productivity among the people in their work environment. He brings to the business table over 20 years of professional experience in career-development counseling and human services.

DeWayne's speaking programs focus on educating, informing, and equipping people with the tools, wisdom and motivation to maximize their productivity in the workplace. He specializes in teaching winning principles and practical approaches to enhance professional and personal growth, while effectively challenging people to think outside of the boxes they have been conditioned to think within. DeWayne is able to get people in the workforce to understand their own value and the incredible value that they bring to their company's success.

Business Name:	Maximum Motivation Training Systems
Address:	PO Box 3531, McKinney, TX 75070
Telephone:	972-547-0840
Email:	dewayne@DewayneOwens.com
Web Address:	www.DewayneOwens.com
Professional Affiliations:	National Speakers Association, North Texas Speakers Association, International Federation for Professional Speakers, American Society for Training & Development

Never give up. No one knows what is going to happen next.

Dorothy in *The Patchwork Girl of Oz*, L. Frank Baum

Kaye Parker

PBBA Atlantic Inc: Think Training

Over 50, But Not Over the Hill

*Your imagination has much to do with your life...it is for you
to decide how you want your imagination to serve you.*

Philip Conley

The following are just a few of the comments I've heard over the last couple of weeks:

"I don't know why they keep me hanging around but they do."

"At my age, I don't dare leave this job. Who would hire me?"

"They wanted me to go for a management position, but I couldn't do that. At least I know what I'm doing in this job."

"I don't know where we are going to find the people to move up the ranks. It's getting harder and harder to find good people."

Women over 50 years of age made the first three comments. The fourth was made by a senior manager. In my opinion, all four of them are missing the boat.

Too many women are selling themselves short. There *are* jobs for women over 50, and you should be applying for those available leadership positions. You have the skills. You have the experience. You have a strong work ethic. You have a loyalty to your organization that just isn't there in today's new employees. If you aren't ready for senior management positions, you can be groomed to be ready. A woman owes it to herself (and her children) to be all she can be.

Furthermore, organizations must wake up to the fact that women over 50 are an untapped source of leadership potential, mentoring material, and sage counsel before it is too late. Once these women have left the workforce, the opportunity is lost. Those who know they have more to offer the business community will go on to start their own business, or they will hang up their skates and let their skills get rusty from lack of use.

As a trainer, facilitator, and consultant, I speak with many employees and senior managers. Their refrain seems to be never-changing and never-ending. On the one hand, there are mature women with enormous potential who are being held back by their own pessimism and defeatist attitudes. On the other hand, there are senior managers, blindly looking past this segment of their workforce, while seeking their leaders from new recruits, who really don't have the experience and the maturity of judgment to take over the reins.

We *can* make our voices heard. Yet we aren't. As an example of what I mean, just look at our political leaders. They are overwhelmingly male. Yes, I do acknowledge that young women have a tremendously important role, bearing the next generation of children. In many families, they still have the greater role, sometimes the only role, in raising them as well. But what is our excuse? Hillary Clinton is over 60, yet she has proven beyond a doubt that mature women have the stamina and the chutzpah to seek political office and give men a good run for their money. Why aren't more women in the running for positions of power, and why aren't more of us supporting those few women who are running?

> There are two ways of spreading light: to be the candle or
> the mirror that reflects it.
>
> Edith Wharton

Women Don't Own Their Value

Why are so many women so self-effacing and unsure of their own value? Three influences shape women's thinking. Let's look at them:

1. Life Influences: First, there is the environment in which we were raised, largely with the input of our mothers. I love my mother dearly and cherish the principles of

Awakening the Workplace

faith, hope, and charity she instilled in me. However, in some ways, these same principles have narrowed my life view. They have created patterns of thinking that I've had to overcome.

>> In my memory, the most sincere compliments I ever received from my mother were when I mastered the art of bread making, when I knitted sweaters for my four brothers and my father one Christmas, and when I planted my first garden, brimming with veggies that I could freeze come fall. The women my mother most admired "kept a neat house," raised "well-mannered children," and "set a good table."

These were very important attributes in my community. Even today, so many years later, I mentally beat myself up if our house is untidy, if one of my grown daughters doesn't remember to send a thank-you card after the Christmas presents are unwrapped, or if I'm unable to pull together some sort of a meal if called upon. They've clearly become part of my operating system that often gets in the way of getting the "real job" done. <<

Since childhood, we have had to learn how to behave with others, and there is nothing to stop us from unlearning and replacing unproductive behaviors at this stage of our life.

2. Organizational Influences: The second influence that has held women back from taking our rightful place at the corporate table are the organizations themselves. The glass ceiling still exists in most companies. If a woman hasn't hit her head against it, it is usually because she hasn't dared to aspire high enough. The not very subtle message is that there should be a male at the head of the corporate table. No, I am not bashing men here. It takes two for that message to stick, and as women, we have been very obliging.

For example, many women often don't see themselves playing a key role in their organizations. They are the invisible leaders, the undervalued support, and the silent wellspring of knowledge about how their organizations work; people who can be our next leaders or the next CEO at the boardroom table. If that role has no appeal, women can lead in other ways, such as through the mentoring of others (more on this later), or through acting in an advisory capacity to those who are willing to take on a leadership role.

3. Self-Perception: The third influence that has held us back, and the one that we can take charge of and have the greatest opportunity to make change is in the way we see ourselves, this being our own self-image and self-esteem. High self-esteem does not mean that we are arrogant, conceited, or insensitive to others' needs. Actually, these traits are more commonly found in people with low self-esteem, as they must build themselves up, even at other people's expense.

Nor does it mean we never have self-doubts. It is probably impossible to go through life without doubting ourselves sometimes. There are times I am almost paralyzed by self-doubt. Nor does high self-esteem protect us from negative thoughts. However, if a woman has a healthy sense of her own self-worth, she can rise above self-criticism. She can have self-doubts without being devastated by them.

If behavior is an outward sign of our inner beliefs, there seem to be many women—especially over 50—who have given up, physically, mentally or emotionally. They've stopped trying to make a difference, and stopping at third base is no different from striking out. The score doesn't change. How we act, or not act, is the basis on which people often make judgments about a person—especially in the workplace. But the fact remains, a person will make judgments based on the behavior that they see, as they have nothing else on which to base their opinions. So being passive in the workplace can be a reflection of your inner sense of self and may lead others to decide that you are not leadership material—as you haven't proven otherwise.

Keys to Moving Ahead—at Any Age

Let's look at some things you can do to make a difference in the workplace and be powerful and influential, regardless of your age:

Learn the Art of Self-Promotion: Women have often taken on the role of making the coffee, taking the minutes, and doing the photocopying, even when men with the same status sit around the boardroom table. A woman often wonders why she isn't being heard. We've not learned the art of self-promotion. We consider it bragging.

>> The first time I banged my fist on a boardroom table to vent my frustration and make my point, I thought the others in the room would have a collective heart attack. Nevertheless, I did make my point and I did get some action on an issue I felt strongly about. <<

This is not about women—especially over 50—starting to bang fists on tables to be heard. What we need to do is to stop accepting being ignored, interrupted, or having our ideas adopted under somebody else's name.

Lead Through Mentoring: While conducting workshops, I ask the participants whether or not they have mentors. The answer is usually "No," and, in fact, many of them don't see the value in mentors. A mentor is someone you consider a role model; someone you can learn from and consult, from time to time, about what options are available and which ones are optimal. A mentor need not be older, male, or in a senior position. He or she just needs to be a person from whom you can learn.

Women in particular seem to think that mentors are only for those who are trying to climb the corporate ladder. This is simply not true. The late president of the United States, Woodrow Wilson, said that he used all the brains he had and all the brains he could borrow. Why would we not take advantage of what other people have learned to help us in our endeavors? Asking someone if they would be one of my mentors is like asking someone to give me a copy of one of their favorite recipes. You always have the option of not using the recipe, or of adapting it to your own particular tastes.

Can you consider being a mentor and serving in an advisory capacity to some of those individuals on their way up? The newspapers are full of stories of people who did not seek wise counsel before they made important decisions. If you could be instrumental in preventing such poor career moves, wouldn't you feel you were providing a valuable service? Few organizations actually think of setting up an advisory council for their fast-track employees, or finding some way to give them the benefit of accumulated knowledge.

Kaye Parker

Learn How to Be Heard: The following is an example from someone I've assisted…

>> Rhonda came to me one day during a series of workshops I was delivering, and said, "How can I get people to listen to me? I have good ideas, but I can't get anyone to listen to them." We talked a little bit further, and she was right. She did have good ideas. In fact, she had great ideas. Yet, I noticed that in these workshops, particularly in small group discussions, her ideas were being drowned out or ignored. And way too soon in the discussion process, she gave up being heard.

She told me this was happening in her workplace, too. In staff meetings, she put forward reasonable, workable ideas, yet they were never discussed. They just died of suffocation, while other ideas—more costly, less time-effective—became the ones the group accepted. It was clear that she was becoming bitter about not having her ideas heard. In her bitterness, she was refusing to acknowledge others' ideas, or give other people credit for their good work. She knew she was being stingy with her praise. She just couldn't bring herself to tell anyone how good their ideas or thoughts were, when she had so many opinions and ideas of her own that nobody was acknowledging. <<

One small part of the solution for Rhonda was to learn how to speak up to be heard. Her voice was soft, and difficult to hear in a heated discussion. For any woman whose voice is too tiny, too soft, or too hesitant, I always suggest they consider going to Toastmasters. This organization, for a nominal yearly fee, gives members many opportunities to speak, and other members will diplomatically help them to "find their voice."

As we talked, Rhonda recognized that she needed to be more giving, more willing to tell others when they did something or said something worthy of praise. However, she had to do more. Rhonda knew she also had to "lower the bar" on what she considered worthy of praise. Some days, just hanging in there is worthy of recognition. She also realized her bitterness was futile and began her own journey by developing and showing a more generous spirit towards herself and with others.

In the remaining few days of the program, I noticed Rhonda smiling more, encouraging other people more, and yet persisting to put her own ideas out for others to hear. It is up to us to put that cycle of reciprocity in motion. What goes around doesn't always come around unless we give things a little push to make them happen.

Realign Your Thinking: We now know that there is not a direct correlation between our self-esteem and our life circumstances. There is another intervening factor that influences self-esteem 100 percent of the time, and that is how you think! When you look in the mirror, does your self-esteem take a beating? Here is what I've discovered:

>> When I look in the mirror and say to myself "I like my hair today" or "I have a friendly looking face," my self-esteem grows. When I look in that same mirror and say to myself, "Kaye, you look like you've been pulled through a knothole backwards," my self-esteem takes a tumble and I immediately feel more tired and haggard. So, I've learned to pay attention to what I tell myself. I CAN change those voices going around in my head, one day at a time. **<<**

Even after years of trying not to, I still put myself down occasionally. Now, when I hear a negative message in my head, I stop and replace it with a new, objective, positive self-statement. You don't need to rely on other people to build your sense of self-worth; it can and should be a do-it-yourself job.

> When you affirm your own rightness in the universe, then you co-
> operate with others easily and automatically as part of your own
> nature. You, being yourself, help others be themselves.
>
> Jane Roberts.

Grow Your Self-Confidence: Genuine self-esteem is the not same as confidence. Real self-confidence is based on the knowledge that you believe in your abilities and believe you will probably be successful at an activity as you have been successful at similar activities in the past.

On occasion, you can pretend to be confident, even when you are not. It helps to remind yourself of past successes. Think of all the things you have done successfully in your life. Write them down and refer to them when you are feeling unsure of your-self or overwhelmed. This list can see you through all sorts of situations.

What is another way of keeping confident and gathering your tattered self-esteem and carrying on? Reminding yourself of great quotations is another tool. I think of Eleanor Roosevelt's famous quotation, "Nobody can make me feel inferior without my permission." It's a phrase I've carried since childhood, and I keep a list of many other ones. You may want to create a list of at least ten powerful quotations and carry them with you. They can help you get through those times when you are being challenged.

Visualization is one technique that I've used successfully to boost my self-esteem and confidence just before stressful events. For example, you have an important presentation to make tomorrow. Rather than imagine all the things that might go wrong, visualize yourself standing tall and competent, sailing through that presen-tation without a single misstep. To make the visual stronger, see yourself in the out-fit you will be wearing, looking professional and confident. Picture the faces that will be in your audience. In your mind's eye, picture them listening with interest, per-haps nodding and smiling if it is appropriate. You can even take visualization one step further and write down a thumbnail sketch of the scene in your head, to anchor it firmly in your mind, and make it more concrete.

Physical Fitness: For any woman over 50 and especially one who wants to be "on her game" at work, this is a must. Physically, I have been doing strength train-ing for a couple of years now and Nordic walking for about the same length of time. The Nordic walking is equally demanding. On Saturday mornings, it is a one-hour, seven-kilometer trek through some hilly terrain, and there are times, especially going up one of those long hills, when I really do want to just quit, take a breather, and saunter back in my own sweet time. The self-discipline to keep going, however, builds both my confidence and my self-esteem.

My resilience after a couple of potentially nasty falls this past year with no more than a few aches and pains was attributed to the strength training I do. It is a chal-lenge, but I like the results. A personal trainer may help, as they are very good at coaxing a bit more effort and keeping you focused.

Mental Stimulation: Our brains age just as our bodies do. However, just as physical exercise can keep our body agile, mental exercise keeps our brain alert. Yes, there is evidence of memory loss after the age of about 40, but that loss is insignificant when we consider all the brain is capable of. Neuroscientists have discovered that stimulating the brain can make it stronger and even stimulate new cells. New learning is not only possible, it can keep the brain young. So go out there and learn a new language or take up bridge.

Mentally, I do crosswords and other word games, always have two or three books on the go, regularly create new workshops for which there is a market, and try to keep up with technology. That last is hardest since I've never been very interested in technology. However, if my business is to grow and prosper, I'd better know what is available and how to use it to my advantage.

Maturity is coming to terms with that other part of yourself.
Dr. Ruth Tiffany Barnhouse

Define Leadership in a New Way: Like many of my friends and colleagues, I've been in business for myself for more than a dozen years now with a successful training, consulting, coaching, and speaking business, and have authored several books. Earning tons of money has never been my driving force (although I am not averse to that). Rather, I can get up each morning motivated and I enjoy going to work. My clients are loyal and they receive good value for my fees. My company can afford to pay me, and my small band of employees, a very decent salary. When I look in the mirror and I *feel* successful, I know that I am a leader.

What does all this have to do with other women over 50 stepping up to the plate and filling that leadership void in their organizations, or starting their own businesses if they choose? The point is that I'm not unique. I'm actually pretty average. Many women are becoming leaders as they define it. The source of being able and willing to do this is determination. In my own sphere of influence, I am determined that I will make use of my experience, determined that I will stay as healthy and as alert as possible so I *can* make use of that experience, and determined that other women can benefit from my experience, and go on to believe in themselves and *their* experiences.

The Next Generation

» Jennie, a woman in one of my workshops this winter, was bewailing the fact that her daughter had decided to embark on a career as a fashion designer. Jennie would have preferred her to start down a more traditional, secure road. "She's bright, smart. Why couldn't she decide to be a lawyer instead?" As mothers, we haven't fallen far from the tree. We want the best for our children, but we want it to be within an environment we know and understand. «

While it is normal to worry about our daughters, we also must applaud their courage when they choose a less-travelled path. While bursting with pride, I can say that both my own daughters are successful in what would be considered non-traditional careers. We owe it to our children to be good role models for them. To show them that we model those bedrock values my mother cherished, and at the same time that we model independent thinking, and are proud of our own self-worth. Let's not rust out, let's wear out, and leave a legacy of positive energy for the women of the future, no matter what age they are.

We need to teach the next generation of children from day one that they are responsible for their lives.

Elisabeth Kübler-Ross

Kaye Parker

Kaye Parker is an optimist. Like Helen Keller, she sees the sunshine, not the shadow. The owner of a successful business in which she coaches, consults, facilitates, trains, and writes, Kaye lives her idea of the perfect job for an optimist.

A former teacher, Kaye has her accreditation with the Canadian Public Relations Society, and her certification from the Canadian Human Resources Association, as well as advanced qualifications to administer and interpret the Myers Briggs Type Inventory. She has trained as a personal efficiency coach, and as a professional recruiter.

In a past venture, Kaye produced and hosted a television program featuring women with interesting lives. Today, she enthusiastically encourages women and the organizations they work for to recognize and put to greater use their talent and their experience. Kaye's workshop participants find her energetic, knowledgeable, and fun. Oh yes, they also find her optimism infectious!

Business Name:	PBBA Atlantic Inc.
Address:	P.O. Box 41108, Dartmouth, NS B2Y 4P7
Telephone:	902-463-8900
Email:	kparker@pbbaatlantic.com
Web Addresses:	www.pbbaatlantic.com
	www.kayeparker.ca
Speaking Affiliations:	Canadian Association of Professional Speakers, Halifax Chapter; Toastmasters International (Schooner Toastmasters)

Only those who risk going too far can possibly find out how far one can go.

T. S. Eliot

Rita Perea

Rita Perea Consulting

Finding the Perfect Coach

You know you're ready for change. You want it! You need it! You're revving your engines to move full speed ahead. But…you aren't sure how to determine your destination, map out your journey, and keep the gas flowing in your engines to get there. So you putter along, moving forward, but not at a rapid pace.

Here is some fantastic news! You can zoom ahead in leadership and life. All you need is assistance from an executive coach like me. An executive coach is a cheerleader and project manager all rolled into one. When you arrive at their office, they help you determine what you want to achieve, map out a path to success, and then cheer you all the way across the finish line. He or she believes you can do it and helps you make it happen.

Hiring a professional coach is an investment in your personal and professional growth. It's recognizing that something needs to change in order to achieve your career aspirations—and that you need help making that change.

According to recently published study results from Manchester Inc., executives who received coaching services realized a sixfold return on their investment. Wow! Imagine achieving almost as much in a single day as you previously did in an entire week—including weekends. How could you not take advantage of these benefits? The most significant improvements came in the area of working relationships (up 77 percent), teamwork (up 67 percent), and productivity (up 53 percent). These results speak for themselves. Working with a coach can truly give you the boost you need to achieve the goals you've always dreamed of, both inside and outside the office.

Coaching isn't for people who have "hit rock bottom." I have some people who come to me feeling overwhelmed or hopeless, but in general, individuals who seek out coaching are truly the best and brightest. They want strategies to help their inner brilliance shine through. Coaching provides customized professional development and heightened personal awareness that no other method can offer.

A word of warning: Coaching is not therapy! The point of coaching is to help you determine where you are at and how to move forward from that point. Coaching is results-oriented. If you need to delve through deep emotional issues from your past, a coach should refer you to the appropriate trained professional for that type of treatment. A qualified, reputable coach will not attempt to solve these types of psychological problems. A coach will help you define and accomplish objectives that can be achieved through behavioral changes and goal setting.

Like any other career development technique, results depend greatly on the quality of the service and the depth of your commitment. You need to be open and ready to challenge your old habits and replace them with new ones. Once you've prepared yourself, following an intentional process for hiring an outstanding coach will help you get the results you want.

What Qualities Belong to a Great Coach?

With any relationship that you enter into, and working with a coach is no exception, you need to look for a defined set of behaviors and qualities:

A Good Questioner: Does this coach ask relevant, probing questions to facilitate the movement of the discussion? Or do you feel that the discussions are circular, on a road leading to nowhere? Great coaches will ask questions that may not be easy to answer but that will cause you to think about your behavior and the changes you want. Professionally trained coaches use specific questioning techniques to help you express your thoughts and feelings. Coaches who lack a solid technique will skip over the deep questioning to tell you what you want to hear or how to accomplish something. Their coaching sessions will feel empty or fluffy, not rich and meaningful.

An Active Listener: Good coaches know when to zip their lips and listen to your celebrations, concerns, hopes, fears, and frustrations. Good coaches will paraphrase what they have heard you say to be sure their understanding is accurate. Professionally trained coaches will use body language—such as nodding, facing you, making eye contact, taking notes—to help you know that they are fully present and engaged in what you say. On the contrary, not-so-good coaches engage in "autobiographical listening," which turns your coaching session into a litany of stories that are all about them and their experiences, not all about you, as it should be. Not-so-good coaches appear distracted, disorganized, and distant. Not-so-good coaches do not accurately remember the details of what you have shared with them.

A Pleasant, Inspirational Demeanor: Great coaches inspire growth and change in their clients. Professional coaches are pleasant and upbeat "people people." They are self-assured and confident without being egotistical. A good coach will delight in your successes and motivate you to move forward. By contrast, not-so-good coaches may produce guilt or anxiety in their clients. Not-so-good coaches may be highly critical and undermine your self-confidence. Not-so-good coaches keep you stuck in the same place.

Ability to Build a Trusting Rapport: When you work with an excellent coach, you will feel safe and at ease. A great coach will work hard at building a trusting relationship that will be the bedrock of your work together. A great coach will go to great lengths to create a confidential, professional, and safe coaching environment. A less-than-professional coach will hold their coaching sessions in a public setting where others may overhear the conversation. Or, worse, they may share too much information about another client with you, which leaves you wondering if your information has been shared too.

Practices Empathy: A great coach will help you feel as though they really, really understand what you are experiencing and how much pain it is causing. A great coach practices empathy, which is the ability to put oneself in another person's spot and understand from their point of view. A not-so-good coach will only tell you what to do or how to do it, without trying to understand your feelings about the situation.

Gently Challenging: Your coach's job is to nudge you gently in the right direction as you work toward reaching your coaching goals. Moving you off square one in a kind, sensitive, and non-critical way is the craft of an excellent coach. Great coaches offer suggestions in a respectful, non-judgmental way. By contrast, a not-so-good coach may be condescending, critical, and aggressive. You may feel bullied into taking actions that may not be in your best interest.

Trustworthy: Excellent coaches demonstrate trustworthiness. They are impeccable with their word. They follow up when they say they will follow up. If they make a promise, they will keep it. They practice speaking their truth and encourage you to do the same. Not-so-great coaches tend to oversell their abilities or expertise just to make money. These coaches may want to keep you "hooked" into their coaching program and will tell you what they think you want to hear. These people generally will not stay in business for very long.

Demonstrate Consistent Behavior: Outstanding coaches demonstrate behaviors that are on an "even keel," and are proactive and consistent. You will not observe crisis-riddled or reactive behaviors in coaches who have it all together. If your coach is experiencing behavioral highs and lows, and sharing their problems with you, they are working out of bounds in the coaching relationship. A coach is there to help you find solutions to your challenges, not the other way around.

Organizationally Adept: Excellent coaches are organized coaches. They show you, by their actions, that they have strong planning and goal-setting skills. They are all about helping you achieve the results you are seeking. They model and help you learn the planning skills you need to reach your goals. Contrast a thorough and organized coach with one who breezes into a meeting late with papers flailing about from their notebook. Which one would you want to put your time and money into?

Results-Oriented Mindset: How does your coach measure your progress toward your goals? Does your coach use surveys or profiles to establish baseline data? All great coaches will gather data in some way to help you determine and reach your goals. Your coach is working for you and you should get transformational results from the resources you have invested in the process.

Intuitive: Coaches who provide wonderful experiences for their clients use their intuition as an inner compass to map the way. Astute coaches guide their clients and facilitate their growth in both the personal and professional arenas by always looking forward to identify and navigate through potential obstacles. Not-so-great coaches may tend to use the "one size fits all approach," rationalizing that if the process worked for one person, it can be put it on autopilot and used with everyone.

Ability to Provide Follow-up Resources: Does your coach give you ideas, book titles, and connections to other people who may help you reach your goals? Does your coach check in with you between coaching sessions? Excellent coaches have outstanding, up-to-date resources that they can easily access and provide to their clients. They have the office support systems in place to do so easily and in a timely manner. Great coaches do what they say they will do, and deliver what you need to keep you moving in the right direction.

Provides Encouragement: Working with a coach is like having your own personal cheerleader. Wonderful coaches provide encouragement by providing a check-in system between coaching sessions. They may phone, email, or send a note of encouragement your way to keep your motivation high as you are practicing your new skills. Likewise, they will want you to reach out to them when you need a little pep talk or booster shot.

Finding a Really Great Coach

Your First Big Decision

Once you have decided that it is time to seek out the services of a coach or personal consultant, your next step is to weigh the options of paying for the coaching services yourself (private pay) or asking your workplace to pay for your sessions (employer funded).

Your employer may provide a coach through a local Employee Assistance Program, either on- or off-site. If you are contemplating a coach funded by your workplace, there are some advantages and disadvantages to consider first. A big advantage with an employer-funded service is that there is no out-of-pocket expense to you as a client. Coaching sessions become a part of your professional growth plan and can occur during work hours. One of the drawbacks of working with a coach paid for by your employer, however, is that the number and length of sessions may be limited. Also, your employer will have the right to certain information, so the confidentiality of your coaching sessions may be compromised. And, your choice of coaches may be restricted.

Choosing to pay privately for the coaching engagement may be more beneficial to you in the end. A possible disadvantage of paying for coaching yourself is that the coach interviewing and selection process may take more time and effort. Another disadvantage is that your personal budget may limit your coach selection. A huge advantage of private-pay services is that it affords the highest degree of privacy and confidentiality. You can share anything with your private-pay coach and it will be kept confidential. Another advantage of self-funded coaching is that you have an unrestricted selection of coaches and an unrestricted range of personal or professional goals to work on achieving. You aren't restricted to the "flavor of the day" initiative at work.

Your Second Big Decision

Now it is time to look at the pros and cons of choosing a coach who works independently versus a coach who works for the same organization that you do. Many large organizations today have coaches on staff to work with their employees. This is an "internal" coach. Cost is an advantage of working with this type of coach. Usually the employer will pay for all of the coaching sessions. Another advantage of working with someone who works for the same organization is that he or she can observe you in many more settings and provide feedback. A disadvantage of working with an internal coach is that you have to deal with a dual work relationship—they are your coach but also your co-worker or maybe even your supervisor. The relationship lines may be a little blurred. The potential for a conflict of interest or a breach of confidentiality is higher with this type of coaching arrangement. Oftentimes, coaches who are also employees lack experience and credibility in working at the senior levels of an organization. They may have a limited perspective.

Engaging an "external" coach—someone who is an independent contractor or consultant—can be advantageous because he or she would naturally have an independent, outside perspective of your issues. They typically are highly skilled and have credibility at the senior management levels. And, a coach who is an independent consultant, and not an employee of your organization, is going to give you greater confidentiality and privacy. Utilizing the services of an external coach might have a few disadvantages. One is that their fees may be a little higher since they have business overhead to cover. Another is that they may not know all of the key players in your workplace and, therefore, give you suggestions that are more general.

In the end, you will need to explore the pros and cons of paying for the coaching yourself or seeking funding from your employer. Will you use the services of an independent coaching professional or a co-worker? Carefully weigh the benefits of each choice and then decide.

Gathering the Names of Possible Coaches

Start your coaching search by asking friends, family members, and associates for referrals. A coach is someone that you will work with on an extended, in-depth basis, so it's important that you feel comfortable with this person. Inquire with people in your network about whether they know of anyone who has hired a coach and what that person experienced. If possible, receive names, contact information, and websites for several reputable professional coaches. You want to have the opportunity to interview several individuals and determine which one is the best fit for you.

Completing Research

Before meeting with coaches, contact them and request an informational brochure or other material about their process, philosophy, and fee structure. Also, if they have a website, read it carefully.

Examine what types of clients the coach serves and what objectives they have achieved. Think about whether their approach would work with your personality. Consider whether you prefer someone with expertise in a particular industry or business setting. Also, determine what meeting schedule and format would work best with your lifestyle and needs. Some people do best with just once-a-week, in-person sessions, while others prefer having 24-hour phone access to a coach.

Also, look into the coach's training. When I hear about coaches hanging out their shingle after completing an online certification, it raises some red flags. The coaching process should be a warm, person-to-person interactive experience, based on well-researched techniques, not a one-size-fits-all, canned approach. The in-depth

Rita Perea

knowledge and ability of a coach is what enables him or her to customize a program to maximize a client's growth. Coaches who have undergone in-person training and have an extensive background offer superior services. Once you've reviewed the promotional material, it's time to get personal!

Preparing to Meet a Coach

Before you complete initial consultations with prospective coaches, you need to think seriously about your level of commitment. By determining what you can and are willing to invest before you make a decision, you can achieve the maximum impact from the experience.

Exercise:

Complete these questions in as much detail as possible prior to meeting your potential coach for the first time:

At the end of a successful coaching engagement, I would like to know and do:

_____

_____

How much time per week am I willing to invest in meeting with my coach and completing tasks assigned?

_____

How much money am I willing to invest for my personal and professional improvement?

_____

When I think about the kind of people that motivate me the most, their qualities include: _____

_____

_____

Awakening the Workplace

Now use these guidelines when meeting with your coach to help you ascertain how well you can work together—and especially how effective the prospective coach will be in helping you meet your goals.

Initial Consultation

Completing an initial consultation can help you determine which coach is the right fit for you. When you contact potential coaches, tell them how you heard about them, and ask to set up a time to talk. Clarify whether they charge for this meeting (many times it's complimentary). Usually you will set up an appointment to speak over the phone or in a face-to-face meeting. In-person consultations give you the opportunity to get to know the person as a whole, which I prefer. But if you and a coach live far apart, a phone conversation can work well.

When interviewing your coach, be sure to ask the right questions. The following are some questions you may want to bring to the meeting or refer to immediately following the consultation:

Questions to ask the coach:
- What is your training?
- Do you hold any special certifications?
- What are your areas of expertise (e.g., executive, business, career)?
- Can you supply client references?
- Do you cap the number of clients you work with at any given time?
- What is your coaching philosophy?
- What are your fees, and what do they include?
- Do you include any special surveys or tools in your coaching process?
- How long would each coaching session last?
- How many coaching sessions do you recommend?
- Do you offer evening or weekend times?
- What is your cancellation policy?
- How do you measure results, and when should I start seeing them?

Questions to ask yourself:

- Does he or she make me feel comfortable?
- Is this someone I could work with on a weekly basis for several months?
- Do I like this person?
- Do they seem knowledgeable about the areas where I need assistance?
- Does their coaching process and format work with my current schedule and commitments?

By the end of your initial consultation, you should clearly know what to expect if you decide to work with this coach. This includes the approach, format, methods, fees, and billing structure. At the end of the first meeting, your coach may ask you to sign a letter of agreement. You certainly don't need to make a decision on the spot; if you're not sure, take your time. You want to go into the coaching process with confidence and enthusiasm—not second guesses.

After seeing so many clients undergo dramatic personal and professional change for the better, I'm confident you'll find the coaching experience as rewarding as I do! Here's one of my favorite examples...

Joshua's Story: Productive at Last!

» *Joshua, a bishop in a large North American religious denomination, was struggling with work–life balance and decided to reach out for help. Joshua discovered me via my website and gave me a call to find out more. We lived in different states, so I offered to conduct a one-hour complimentary initial phone consultation. During our conversation, I shared my beliefs and philosophy about the coaching process. I also told Joshua that I used surveys and profiles to assist us in establishing goals and moving forward in a more efficient manner.*

Joshua and I connected easily and quickly over the phone. Plus I was certified in the area of work–life balance, so we promptly agreed to a series of 12 coaching sessions. At the end of our dozen calls, Joshua saw tremendous results in his personal and professional productivity. No longer did he go home from work exhausted and feeling as though he had accomplished nothing. He now felt productive! Capable! At the top of his game! «

By investing in his future and opening himself up to learn and practice new skills, Joshua's career and relationships began to soar. Joshua checks in with me a couple of times a year, and I'm so proud of him and the results he's achieved! Now, two years later, Joshua has advanced to a different position within his denomination and is sustaining a long-term relationship for the first time in many years. He tells me he's never felt better or been happier in his life. Now that's results!

Hiring Your Coach

By now, you have determined which coach and coaching arrangement can best fit your needs. You also know how many coaching sessions your new coach is recommending, and how long your coaching engagement will last. Now it is time to look at the coaching contract. This document will outline all of the important highlights of the coaching engagement, what your responsibilities are, and what your coach's responsibilities are. Pay careful attention to the fee section in the contract so you know exactly what you should receive and how much you are required to pay.

A Word About Fees

Professionally trained, experienced coaches should be viewed as an investment in your personal and professional growth. Coaches have invested in their own education to receive the academic and real-life training to perform their craft well. There are as many different fee structures as there are coaches. You can expect to pay approximately $250–$350 per coaching session for a high-quality coach who has been in the business for a long time. Be sure to understand how long each coaching session will last. Some coaches run 50-minute coaching sessions; some meet with clients for up to two hours per session. Be clear about how much you will be paying for your coach, on average, per hour. Also, find out if your coach charges extra or if follow-up, email, phone calls, and surveys are included in their base rate. What are the terms of the coaching arrangement? Does your coach ask you to pay a certain percentage of the fee after each session? Are you being asked to make a 50 percent down payment up front? If so, when will the remaining 50 percent be due? You would not purchase a home without having it inspected. You would not sign a mortgage without understanding all of the contract details. The same is true when making an investment in a coach. Be sure that you are operating with a clear understanding prior to beginning your first session together.

Now, Get Coached!

Congratulations! You've done your homework. You have pinpointed the qualities you are seeking in a coach. You have interviewed some highly recommended individuals and have found one you believe can really help you reach your goals. You've found the right person to guide you on your journey and you'll be able to move full speed ahead toward your dreams. The flag has dropped and it's time for you to zoom forward over the finish line! Are you ready? Fasten your seat belt. On your mark, get set, go!

Rita Perea

Rita Perea brings a powerful blend of passion and professionalism to both private and public sector organizations as the founder of Rita Perea Consulting. As a consultant, coach and keynote speaker, she shares her 20-plus years of experience with hundreds of leaders annually in organizations ranging from Fortune 500s and high-tech startups to not-for-profits. Clients who have engaged her services include teams and individuals from Nationwide Insurance, Team Quest International, and Meredith Corporation, just to name a few.

Rita holds both a bachelor's and master's degree, and also a specialist's degree in leadership. She specializes in working with young professionals who aspire to leadership positions, as well as successful leaders transitioning into a new organization or upward into significantly more challenging levels of leadership. Rita holds several certifications, including communications and work-life integration specialist.

Rita is the author of the soon-to-be released *From Frantic to Fabulous: Designing the Life You Deserve* (2008). She and her physician-husband, Ernie, reside in the heartland of America, Des Moines, Iowa. They adore international travel, fine dining, and providing service to those who are less fortunate.

Business Name:	Rita Perea Consulting
Address:	1200 Valley West Drive, Suite 304-12
	West Des Moines, IA 50266
Telephone:	515-577-5666
Email:	Rita@RitaPerea.com
Web Address:	www.RitaPereaConsulting.com
Professional Affiliations:	National Speakers Association; American Society of Training and Development; Society for Human Resource Managers; Rotary International.

Real knowledge is to know the extent of one's ignorance.

Confucius

Edree Allen-Agbro

Interpersonal Skill Coaching

Crack the Conflict Codes at Work and Reap the Rewards

Have you or someone you know ever experienced any of the following?

- Spent half the day dealing with conflict among your employees?
- Stayed at home to avoid conflict with someone at work?
- Felt intense anger, tension, or even fear because of conflict at work?
- Had trouble getting things done because of tension and lack of co-operation?
- Threatened someone, or felt intimidated or threatened by someone in your workplace?

It would be surprising if you could not identify with at least one of these experiences. Workplace conflict is widespread, destructive, and costly in many ways. In the literature concerning workplaces, conflict-related stress is referred to as astronomical and epidemic in proportion, "the disease of the century."

Ironically, the parallel trend is that of co-operation. To be truly competitive in today's global work environment, leaders and workers must have strong *co-operation* skills. For example, some Fortune 500 companies have added relationship building and collaboration skills as a top priority for everyone they hire.

The good news: Conflict is a naturally occurring outcome when people with different perspectives, priorities, and goals interact in the work environment. The presence of conflict is nobody's fault. There is no one to blame.

The even better news: The negative effects of conflict are not inevitable. If conflict is handled well, it can become a catalyst for greater co-operation, more creative and effective solutions, and a healthier, more profitable environment.

The best news of all: There is a natural path from conflict to co-operation that is accessible and effective. It involves waking up to the true nature and constructive potential of conflict. It also involves becoming more conscious about how you interact with others around conflict. It involves cracking and rewriting the code. The codes are the underlying principles, patterns, and practices that cause the system of conflict to be maintained. Instilling new codes can transform the workplace and accelerate the growth of healthier, more satisfying, productive, and profitable workplace experiences.

Understanding the Nature of Conflict

We have many myths about conflict that directly impact how a person responds to it. Let's debunk those myths and look at some of the truths about conflict:

- **Conflict is not evil**. Conflict occurs naturally when two or more differences (in perspectives, intentions, values, goals, for example) collide. It is like the sparks that fly when the chemicals on the end of a matchstick strike the rough edge of a matchbox.
- **Conflict is not essentially dangerous.** Conflict can be creative. When conflict is handled well, the differences between people can lead to better decisions, better solutions, and far greater outcomes.
- **Conflict is not limited to isolated events.** Conflict is part of interrelated systems of ideas, interactions, and practices. In other words, the quality and outcomes depend on how you and others at work think, talk, act, and feel.
- **Conflict is not one party's "fault."** Looking for someone to blame is a total waste of time and energy. It misses the systemic elements that could help you understand the conflict. It also steals the focus from harnessing the creative possibilities hidden in the conflict.
- **Conflict can be transformed into co-operation.** By becoming conscious and shifting how you think, act, communicate, and feel, you and others you work with can transform conflict into co-operation.

Cracking the Four Conflict Codes

The following is the core of an approach designed and developed by myself and proven highly successful with hundreds of clients. I call it the "Four Conflict Codes." It is based on scientific and professional evidence, over 20 years of experience, and dramatic results with hundreds of clients. You are being invited to wake up, crack the four conflict codes, and transform those sparks of conflict from harmful and destructive to warm and enlightening. The four conflict codes are:

1. **The Mindset Code:** How people habitually *think* in the workplace;
2. **The Behavior Code:** How people *act* toward and with each other at work;
3. **The Conversation Code**: How people *communicate* with each other and about each other;
4. **The Emotion Code**: The *feelings* people bring to and cultivate in the workplace.

Each appears and unfolds in its own way in the workplace. We'll look at each in more detail, with suggestions for how to solve the problems that each addresses.

Conflict Code # 1—Mindset Code

Is Your Code "Work as War"? Shift That Metaphor!

» In the fall of 2001, during an extremely stressful time in United States history, I co-facilitated a three-day retreat of early childhood educators from across the US. They were deeply concerned about the impact of violence and harsh reality on their "gentle profession" of developing young children.

At first, they strongly resisted my suggestion that their daily thoughts and behaviors at work might be warlike. My comments rubbed against their professional self-images and caused some conflict. But being open learners, they decided to explore the question. When I asked them to identify the war analogies they used on a daily basis, they began to wake up to how pervasively they thought, talked, and worked like warriors.

For example, they discovered that the language of war was rampant in their workplace. They spoke of their work with families and small children as being "in the trenches." They mentioned having to "pick their battles," and of feeling "under siege." Their brainstorming got so lively that I jokingly begged them to slow down so I could record the "bullet points" on the flip chart. **«**

> *The concepts that govern our thoughts are not just a matter*
> *of the intellect… Our concepts govern what we perceive,*
> *how we get around in the world, and how we relate to*
> *other people.*
>
> George Lakoff and Mark Johnson,
> *Metaphors We Live By* (1980)

It is not about declaring "war" on the conscious war mindset, nor choosing co-operation over competition. There are times when the war mindset is appropriate. The point is that when the war mindset is the unconscious default viewpoint, a person is not consciously choosing how to respond. In turn, we *separate from* rather than *connect with* each other. Rather than influence, you can antagonize. And a person can "go for the jugular" when really he or she is trying to help.

When the war mindset is the primary one operating at work,
it contributes to ongoing destructive conflict
and makes true co-operation difficult or impossible.

The war mindset is the default pattern at your workplace if:

- Work groups tend to view each other as enemies they have to fight or defend against (for example, labor versus management, production versus sales, field versus headquarters, or programmers versus testers);
- Individuals or work groups view themselves as all right and the other as all wrong;
- People are expected to take "sides" and are suspect if they seem open to the other side's perspective;

- People use war language regularly and rarely or never question it;
- Conflict gets worse, not better. "Resolved" conflict goes underground. Existing conflict escalates and tensions increase;
- People get "worked up" at the thought of doing "battle" with another work group;
- Joining with another company feels like a "hostile takeover."

Shift the "Work as War" Mindset!

Exercise 1

Become more aware that **war** is the unconscious metaphor you participate in at work. Ask yourselves:

A. Do different work groups ever speak of each other or act as if they are enemies?

B. How much do I/we unconsciously talk about work matters as if we are at war? For example, do our marketing people sharpen their marketing "weapons" to use on "target markets?"

Exercise 2

A. Brainstorm the use of war language and talk about how it plays out daily.

B. Choose another metaphor to describe your workplace. One of the popular metaphors my clients choose is gardening. What would your workplace be like if you approached work as if it were a garden instead of a battleground? Another metaphor is an orchestra with the leader as conductor and each musician and section working literally in harmony.

Exercise 3

Practice consciously selecting a metaphor that serves you better to frame the way you work.

- How would you think about the work, yourself, and all other stakeholders (clients, vendors, leaders, investors, and so on) based on the new metaphor?
- How would everyday language change?
- What alternatives to "battles and trenches" would pepper daily conversation?

- How would the energy at work shift?
- What are the likely outcomes of your new metaphor?

Conflict Code #2—Behavior Code

Is Your Code a Set of Polarizing Behaviors?
Recycle Those Behaviors!

How do you feel when you are asked to learn new information and skills at work? Do you ever feel overwhelmed by trying to stop doing the "wrong" behaviors and start practicing the "right" ones, while keeping up with your current workload and responsibilities?

It is necessary to learn new perspectives and behaviors in order to transform conflict into co-operation. However, it is also possible to build on already habitual behaviors. Some behaviors that are traditionally seen as negative and polarizing can surprisingly be redirected in order to transform conflict.

Some habits are universal but, in many cultures, are seen as negative. Gossiping, stereotyping, and jumping to conclusions are actually neutral. However, the content can be negative or positive. Let's focus, for example, on gossip as a useful "bad" habit.

Recycle Destructive Old Gossip Behavior

Human beings are essentially storytellers. And one of our favorite story subjects to tell and hear about is other people. This is called gossip. Gossip is used as informal orientation—to teach people "what is and is not acceptable around here." It also serves to test our own behavior against other people and the opinions that matter to us. However, as you know, gossip can quickly get out of hand and become very destructive in the workplace. Destructive gossip stems from the War Metaphor mindset. Gossip at work contributes to destructive conflict when the gossipers:

- Have conscious or unconscious harmful intentions;
- Spread stories that have damaging content;
- Selectively share the gossip with others who are inclined to make it worse;
- Spread the kind of gossip that contributes to an environment of low trust.

The way to recycle destructive gossip is to use the "grapevine" as a communication channel and change the content to constructive or "good" gossip. Gossip is constructive when the gossipers:

- Have consciously constructive intentions;
- Share what they appreciate about the person being gossiped about—the "gossipee";
- Refrain from spreading private information about others;
- Spread the kind of gossip that if the person being gossiped about were to hear it, it would make their day.

Exercise 1

Think about someone at work that you could appreciate a bit more than you do now. Imagine how spreading good gossip about the person could improve your work relationship with them. Start to notice what you genuinely appreciate about them.

Exercise 2

Fill in the blanks of this hypothetical positive gossip planner. (Yes, a gossip planner! It's part of becoming more conscious.) Using the guidelines in Exercise 1, fill in the blanks with constructive comments.

Good Gossip Planning Worksheet

You (as gossip sender, in a hushed tone): *Do you believe what _____ did yesterday?*

Gossipy colleague (gossip receiver): *No, What did s/he do?*

You: *I can't believe it! I could barely wait to tell you.*

Gossipy colleague: I can't stand it. What did s/he do?

You: *Well, remember last week in the Positive Communications class, we learned that we should_____?*

Gossipy colleague: Yes. Wait. I don't believe it. Did s/he…?

You: *Yes, s/he did! This morning, s/he came to me and asked if we could talk. S/he _____ how I felt about _____. S/he _____ my feelings and actually _____!*

Gossipy colleague: That is unbelievable.

You: *Okay, I have to get back to work. Don't tell anybody.*

Gossipy colleague: Don't worry. I won't.

Gossipy colleague (on the phone to someone else): You'll never believe what _____ did. S/he has gone stark raving positive! I'm not supposed to tell, but she is really _____.

Conflict Code #3—Communication Code

Is Your Code to Debate and Discuss
When You Need to Dialogue? Choose Dialogue!

» A school brought me in to facilitate a dialogue. They were very concerned about a conflict that had been brewing for literally several years. It finally reached a peak and could no longer be ignored. It was not going to go away. It was only getting worse. So I worked with the sponsor and the committee to clarify the issue, the needs, and the goals. My strategy for guiding clients through conflict to co-operation combines self-reflection (the waking-up element) and skills development, as well as the actual conversations.

I met separately with each group—the students on one hand and the staff and faculty on the other. During the periods of self-reflection, it became clear to the students that although they said they wanted dialogue, deep down inside they wanted to win—in order to "nail" the faculty and staff by blaming them and showing them how "wrong" they were.

The faculty and staff also had a chance privately to uncover their own "deeply hidden agendas." They realized that one of the reasons they had put off the conversation for so long was because they were afraid they would be "attacked" by the students. They were afraid of being labeled and ostracized as prejudiced and bad. «

Both sides were asking for dialogue. Both sides had been preparing for verbal war. They said they wanted dialogue. What they really wanted, unconsciously, was a debate.

Three Communication Styles: Debate, Discussion, and Dialogue

There are the three main types of conversation that most people at work engage in. Each one has its own:

- Structure;
- Underlying assumptions;
- Purposes;
- Goals;
- Strategies;
- Likely outcomes.

The problem occurs when the conversation styles are unconscious and automatic. For example, most lawyers are trained and paid to be warriors. They have to become unconsciously competent at the skills of debate.

>> During a chat with a partner in a prestigious law firm, we touched on the subject of interpersonal skills for lawyers. I voiced my professional opinion by saying, "You can be excellent at arguing a point and brilliant at winning a lawsuit. But those skills will not help you build relationships." He chuckled, "That's what my wife tells me all the time." «

The differences between the three communication styles may seem subtle, but they have profound consequences in issues of conflict and co-operation.

Debate Style

It has been shown that this is one of the most common unconscious default styles. This one is more closely aligned with the War Metaphor than the other two.

- The *content* consists of *ideas* and *facts* to back up ideas;
- The *purpose* of a debate is to *win* and beat the other side;
- The *relationship* of the two sides is as *opponents*;
- The *strategy* is to *attack* their ideas or arguments and *defend* your own arguments by proving superiority;
- The *reason for listening* to the other side is to *uncover weakness*, both in their ideas and in their confidence;

- The *feeling atmosphere* is generally *tense* and *lively*;
- The *likely outcome* is *polarization*.

People rarely end a debate by having persuaded the other party to their side. There will likely be hurt feelings. If the debate is formal and intentional, the party that lost might feel only disappointment. However, in the workplace, the feelings are likely to be more intense and enduring.

Discussion Style

This is another very common conversation style in many workplaces.
- The *purpose* of a discussion is to *exchange ideas*;
- The *relationship* is as *colleagues, acquaintances,* or *friends*;
- The *strategy* is to *volley*, simultaneously or sequentially, and sometimes *explore* the ideas further;
- The *purpose for talking* is to *persuade, decide* or sometimes to *impress* and *entertain*;
- The main *reason for listening* is to *find an opportunity to contribute your ideas*;
- The *content* is mostly *ideas, facts,* and *opinions*;
- The *feeling atmosphere* can be *mild* or *lively* and sometimes *heated*, depending on the subject matter;
- The *likely outcome* is some form of *status quo*. People usually leave a discussion without deeply changed ideas or beliefs.

A colleague once described a discussion as two people or groups throwing an "idea discus" at each other like the sport.

Dialogue Style

Dialogue is the least common mode of conversation yet the most likely to transform conflict into co-operation.
- The *purpose* of a dialogue is to *understand, be understood,* and *connect*;
- The *relationship* is first as *people*;
- The *strategy* is to *share, inquire, empathize, acknowledge* and *listen*;
- The main *reason for listening* is to *understand* the other person better, and to *look for* both *common ground* and *interesting differences*;

- The *content* includes *feelings, experiences,* and appropriate *personal* (not necessarily private) *information;*
- The *feeling atmosphere* is usually *open, dynamic,* and eventually a *relief;*
- The *likely outcomes* include increased *mutual understanding, deeper self-understanding, new, shared meaning,* and more *clarity* about the work relationship and the work.

Choose Dialogue Power for Co-operation

Exercise 1

Start to observe your co-workers in conversation. Practice noticing if they are mostly debating, discussing, or engaging in dialogue. Compare the outcomes they are trying to reach with the style of conversation they are using. What do you observe?

Exercise 2

Create a conscious plan for an important conversation that is already on your calendar. Alternatively, think of an important work relationship that you could improve with good dialogue.

With the help of a coach or skillful communicator, or your own quiet resources, go through the following 10-point checklist to plan your part of a dialogue.

Dialogue Checklist

1. What is my true purpose for wanting this conversation?
2. How would I describe our current work relationship?
3. How would I like to us improve it? Why is this important to me?
4. Am I really willing to listen to this person, without judging them?
5. How am I curious about this person's ideas and their experience of the work or their experience of working with me?
6. What do I appreciate about them that I've never let them know?
7. What do I want them to know about me?

8. What do I need to share with them about me that could improve our work relationship? What am I willing to share about me as a person?

9. Am I as open to being influenced by what they say as I am interested in persuading them?

10. What else do I need to plan in order to make this a great conversation? Timing? Pleasant, mutually agreeable setting? Anything else?

Conflict Code #4—Emotion Code

Is Your Code the "Negative Emotions" Code?
Release Those Negative Emotions!

» It was great seeing my former colleague again after such a long time. We sat in the quaint Cuban-style coffeehouse on a hill near downtown Seattle. She filled me in on what was happening in the old workplace.

We were both startled by my sudden outburst of sadness and tears as she related a story to me about what a part-time employee was experiencing. Hearing about her experiences triggered the last residual feelings about my own painful experience at that workplace.

Luckily, we were tucked away in a cozy alcove, so the presence of other customers did not interrupt my need to get it out of my system. The way my colleague responded was brilliant. It transformed my inner conflict—feelings I didn't realize were still there—into co-operation with my conscious decision to "let it go."

She silently and supportively let me cry. Without judging me or the other people involved, she used her marvelous listening skills. When I had calmed down and my tears subsided, she did something remarkable. She reached across the table, took both of my hands, and apologized to me on behalf of the organization for having experienced that pain. It was so healing. «

Though I had worked to release my feelings and judgments and done some journaling about forgiveness, I still had hurt feelings. What was missing was the other half of the forgiveness equation: an apology.

My friend's apology was perfect. She didn't even work there when the incident occurred. As a surrogate, her apology may have been even more powerful for me than one from people directly involved, for the following reasons:

- I trusted her and had no reason to feel suspicious of her motives for apologizing;
- She had no investment in needing to justify or defend any part of the hurtful behavior, including the lack of a previous apology;
- Because she was not involved in any way, my emotions didn't trigger any negative feelings about myself;
- It was virtually impossible for me to receive an apology from the people actually involved.

Emotions, Apologies, and Letting Go

Emotions are perhaps the most essential aspect of conflict in the workplace. One of the greatest mistakes most people make is to underestimate or ignore the power that emotions have.

- Emotions are an essential part of conflict. Strong feelings are both part of the catalyst for conflict and outcomes of conflict;
- Negative emotions, such as anger, shame, fear, hatred, and humiliation, tend to increase when the thoughts, communication, and behavior surrounding conflict is adversarial;
- Many emotional "hidden agendas" are really "*deeply* hidden agendas." This means the person is not consciously aware of these feelings and how they are affecting their behavior;
- Most hidden feelings have grown over time. They are old hurts from past conflicts that have not been completely released;
- Lingering negative emotions create a stressful work environment and contribute to the terrible human and financial costs of conflict;
- Transforming conflict includes healing old and current hurts.

Release Those Negative Emotions

The complementary actions of apology and forgiveness are profound. They accelerate the journey from conflict to co-operation by transforming the energy of negative emotions. Know you may need help with this. Start to use these powerful tools gently by applying them to conflict at your workplace.

Exercise 1

Listen respectfully the next time a colleague or client tells a story of a past or existing workplace pain. If you truly feel sorry that they have had this painful experience, tell them. If appropriate, apologize on behalf of the organization, or the profession—or just as a fellow human being.

Exercise 2

Find a way to forgive anyone from your past or present work situation; let go of the feelings that eat you up This does not mean that you should excuse what they did or condone the actions. Get a coach, advisor, therapist, or trusted friend to help you do this.

Become a Powerful Conflict Transformer at Work

Your workplace—and the world—needs conflict transformers. Both conflict and co-operation are part of our natural programming. What we have as our human birthright is the capacity to choose and shape our world and work according to those choices.

The conflict that happens in your work is a perfect opportunity to awaken those choices. You and your colleagues can crack the four conflict codes and rewrite them to create a more co-operative, productive, and humanely profitable environment. Choose now to crack:

- the *Mindset Code* by shifting from thinking of "work as war" to work as a place that cultivates the co-operative human spirit;
- the *Behavior Code* by behaving as if what you have with others in the workplace is a common humanness and the purpose of the work, and as if your

differences can generate new possibilities rather than tear you apart;

- the *Conversation Code* by adding true dialogue to the possible ways you communicate with each other; and
- the *Emotion Code* by consciously choosing to cultivate the kinds of feelings that make people glad when the workweek begins.

Tap into and develop your natural ability to think, feel, communicate, and act in ways that generate true co-operation. Reap and share the benefits!

Edree Allen-Agbro

Edree Allen-Agbro's earliest memory of coaching leaders was at age four, when she lovingly challenged her favorite "Uncle Honey" about a gap between his words and his actions. He later confided that her "intervention" inspired him to make positive life changes.

Building on this early success, and with her education in behavioral science and adult learning, Edree has spent 30 years as an interpersonal skills coach, consultant and leadership trainer. She has developed unique and engaging methods for mastering emotional and social intelligence. These include her original Conflict Transformation Dialogues™ and her Interpersonal Fitness Coaching™ programs.

Working in both the public and private sectors, Edree has guided senior management and their staff to transform conflict and raise their interpersonal skills to stay on top of their game. Clients include corporations, such as Microsoft and Hewlett Packard, as well as school districts, universities, and social service agencies.

Edree keeps her own interpersonal muscles toned and happy with the heat of Latin dancing and the coolness of jazz.

Business Name: Interpersonal Skill Coaching
Address: 2606 2nd Avenue, Suite 335, Seattle, WA 98121
Telephone: 206-374-7446
Email: edree@edreeallenagbro.com
Web Address: www.conflicttransformer.com

Photo: Ingrid Pape-Sheldon Photography

Anne Baldwin

One Step Consulting

Avoiding the Superwoman Trap

Clearly, I recall how thinking about the Superwoman Trap began. While driving home one day, my 10-year-old son asked one of his typical thought-provoking questions. "Mom," he asked, "if you could have superhero powers, which ones would you want to have?" I remember answering, without really thinking, that I would like to be able to fly, or to have elastic arms, or be invisible, or some equally thrilling talent. Although I answered quickly and glibly, it truly was an "aha" moment for me—the moment was so profound I slammed on the car brakes and sent us lurching forward. As Edna, in the Walt Disney superhero movie *The Incredibles*, stated to Elastic Girl, "What are you talking about, darling?!" My realization was that:

>> Every day I behaved as if I had superhero powers—albeit not as exciting as flying or reading minds. I continually set expectations for myself that only someone with super powers would be capable of. In my case, though, it was not for a rare crisis—like Superman rescuing Lois from a rock slide—that I was leaving behind my real identity and taking on a superhero persona to swoop in and right the world with my talents and flashy cape and costume. On the contrary, this was a standing agenda item in my world; something I expected of myself everyday, 24 hours a day, and often 365 days a year. «

At the time my son asked this question, I was working full-time, often traveling out of town, as well as organizing and coordinating registration for soccer and basketball for our community. In addition, I coached the three basketball teams of my children, was a team mom for soccer, and was doing preparations for the dance show. At the same time, I was committed to physical fitness for myself and, oh yes, let's not forget about being a loving wife and mother at all times…

Some of these tasks that I had agreed to I still enjoyed; however, for many of the activities I found myself doing, I no longer even evaluated if I was enjoying myself. Doing and performing this many activities had just become my natural way of being. So basically, after a minimum 40+ hour week in my "real" profession, about 2000 sports registrations, and endless hours on the fields and in the dressing rooms, I came to the realization that I was spiraling out of control.

Somewhere along the way, I had lost myself and I had taken on the persona of a superhero! How had this happened? Even though I am a well-rounded and strong person, who knows herself well, I realized that saving the day had become a routine occurrence, to the point where I finally realized I needed to save myself. Clearly, I had fallen into the Superwoman Trap and I did not even notice how or when it had occurred.

The Superwoman Trap

The Superwoman Trap is characterized by the need to take on too much, the need to do too much, the need to be busy all the time, and for many women, the need to do everything and be everywhere. The Superwoman Trap leaves you s-t-r-e-t-c-h-e-d beyond what is humanly possible.

Now, I am not talking about a happy, buzzing kind of busy. That is the kind of busy when you have a big deadline at work or an important event in your home life and you are working toward achieving that goal. You have it mapped out and are aware of the work and tasks that need to be accomplished. You are confident that the goal is achievable and you almost enter a trance-like state as you get into a rhythm working toward the goal—and most importantly, it is fun! You may be working within a team or independently. Either way, synergy is at work and the fast pace is exhilarating and your adrenalin is flowing. The key point in being happy-busy is that it is a sporadic or special event that you gear up for, and although it is a bit crazy for a few days here and there, it also includes a sense of excitement about working toward the goal and feeling good about yourself as things all come together. You know this crazy pace has a definite end date, after which life will return to the normal-busy but manageable pace.

The Superwoman Trap is when you move from that sporadic adrenalin feeling to a consistent day-to-day full superhero firing on all cylinders experience—each and every day. It may start as the "buzzing busy" feeling; however, as the expectation to keep up this pace becomes prolonged, the productive rhythm changes. With the continuing high expectations, you may begin to feel that you never have room for error. There is no end that you can see without falling short of everyone's expectations, particularly your own. You know the feeling; you probably have experienced it yourself and most certainly have witnessed the phenomenon in your colleagues or friends. Just listen to how women talk to each other about being busy—"crazy busy." Gone are the days of just enjoying. Now, we say it is "all good," regardless of the fact that it quite certainly is *not* all good.

» As I was beginning the journey of recognizing this phenomenon in myself, my colleague's experience affirmed my thoughts. Sandi and I had been work colleagues for 15 years, seeing each other every two to three months as we progressed in our careers and home lives. I had always marveled at how efficient she was and I was amazed at her ability to be a superwoman without ever seeming to miss a beat.

When I saw her this time at a conference, we exchanged pleasantries and air kisses and proceeded to catch up from where we had left off last time. As we chatted about what we were focusing on at work and with new projects, I had to comment to her that she looked fabulous. Sandi, in fact, looked radiant, although there was nothing in particular different about her. I was amazed at her response. Sandi informed me that she had not changed her hair or her wardrobe; what had changed was her expectation of herself—and that had changed her life.

She proceeded to tell me that she had been feeling more and more stressed and unfulfilled each day and it finally took a medical episode to convince her that drastic changes had to me made. When I commented that she always seemed so capable and unfrazzled by any event, she laughed and said that was the persona she took on. It was never really her and she had finally realized that she was tired of being "a super-woman." **«**

We'll look at how Sandi had solved this superwoman dilemma a little later. First, here is an assessment tool to help you see if—and how far—you've fallen into the Superwoman Trap.

10 Signs of Falling Into the Superwoman Trap

1. Do you frequently find yourself agreeing to take on more work or do more, even though you already feel overloaded?
    [ ] Yes [ ] No
2. Do you frequently catch yourself thinking, "In my next life…"?
    [ ] Yes [ ] No
3. Do you frequently find yourself thinking, "I will stop doing so much once this project is done… right after I finish this…?"
    [ ] Yes [ ] No
4. Do you consistently overbook your day?
    [ ] Yes [ ] No
5. Do you often start your day already feeling behind?
    [ ] Yes [ ] No
6. Do you consistently make decisions because you feel guilty that you should be doing this or that?
    [ ] Yes [ ] No
7. Do you consistently make decisions based upon fear rather than feelings of opportunity?
    [ ] Yes [ ] No
8. Do you do so much because you are afraid of being left out or missing something if you say "No" or slow down?
    [ ] Yes [ ] No
9. Do you equate being busy as being valued and needed?
    [ ] Yes [ ] No

10. When things do not work out, do you find yourself disproportionately upset or angry?

[ ] Yes [ ] No

If you have answered "Yes" to 1–3 of these questions:
  Well done! You are managing your busy schedule.
If you answered "Yes" to 3–5 of these questions:
  You are at risk of falling into the Superwoman Trap
If you answered "Yes" to 5–10 of these questions:
  You are in the Superwoman Trap. Read on!

So what is to be done? If you have read the above scenarios and suspect or know that you are falling into the Superwoman Trap, do not be alarmed—you are not alone! So, what leads a woman to falling into the Superwoman Trap?

Because we can—and we are expected to: The wonderful thing about modern society is that we have all these conveniences that are supposed to make our lives easier and less busy or less difficult. These are the cell phones, email, instant messaging, laptops and computers, automatic everything, from cars to can openers to pepper shakers, microwave ovens, fast food, deli food—the list goes on and on. However, many of these so-called liberating technologies often feed into our belief that we can do more and we have to do more as we have more time, more options, more energy, or just more everything. These modern conveniences lull us into thinking that we can be superheroes weekly, daily, or hourly—basically constantly. Yet, the reality is, we still only have about 16 hours each day to accomplish all the tasks we have committed ourselves to. Remember, a superhero only takes on the "wonder" persona or identity on rare occasions, not 24/7.

When I go to our cottage on the lake each summer, I'm reminded of how I have become accustomed to doing multiple tasks all the time. As it is an older cottage, the phone attached to the wall is a relic. Not being able to walk around and multitask while on the phone is almost more than I can bear some days, and yet I am on the phone for no more than 3 to 5 minutes at a time. And I can imagine what I must look like stretching that cord to its full length and leaning as far as I can to be able to pick up a T-shirt or cup. Clearly, I think I have elastic superhero arms despite consistent evidence to the contrary! And really, why do I not just concentrate on the phone call for the few brief minutes that I am on the phone?

"Busy" is believed to be a badge of honor: Following right along with "because we can," many women get caught up in the "superhero replication act." We perceive that all of our colleagues or friends seem to be managing to be super-heroes on a regular basis, so we believe this illusion as being the new normal. I can recall many incidences where I have heard colleagues talking about being involved in Toastmasters, taking MBA courses, and leading new projects and initiatives at work, and before I know it, I find myself throwing on my superhero cape and tur-bocharged boots with my mind racing as to how I can fit all this in.

The problem is not so much my contemplation of taking on these additional roles or tasks. The problem lies in the fact that I had never considered these impor-tant to me before someone else mentioned them, and yet I am again assuming superhuman prowess to accomplish something that, until that moment, was not even on my radar of what matters!

Guilt is in control: Most superheroes don their identity to save the world from a villain or to prevent a disaster, not because they have to, but because they feel they need to. Many of us seem to have this heightened level of social responsibility tied to our identity, combined with a lack of clarity about what matters to us in our own lives, which fuels the need to take on these superhuman roles. We feel guilty if we do not volunteer for everything, even though we do not really want to be doing these tasks. Combined with taking on items that are clearly more than any person can accomplish, it is just a recipe for feeling guilty when we cannot accomplish it all. The irony is that, instead of realizing we're acting like a superhero, this guilt make us more determined to take on more next time as we are sure we can do it all!

We enjoy being perceived as wonderful: I must admit I suffer from this myself from time to time, even now. Tied into the lack of clarity about what is important to us, many of us enjoy the initial accolades we receive for agreeing to take on so many tasks or roles. The admiration we repeatedly receive propels us to continue to take on the superhero role and we become addicted to the external admiration, however superficial and fleeting.

We become superheroes to avoid self-reflection: For many of us, this is the most common and yet the most serious reason for becoming superheroes. As we amass many roles and expectations of ourselves—as often happens insidiously over time—we lose sight of who we are as individuals, without even realizing it. We lose sight of what is important to us and to those key people around us. The role of working woman combined with mother, daughter, friend, wife, or whatever roles we have taken on, somehow has left us busy, but we are not sure for what. As a result, just continuing to take on more in an effort to "save the world" seems easier than having to pause and examine our own lives. Such examination would require us to evaluate if we are happy, fulfilled, and moving forward with what is really important in our lives.

A buffet of all of the above: If you are like me, the reasons for being a superhero combine a little of all of the above, depending on the situation! I enjoy the accolades for being so wonderful and doing all these things for strangers or mere acquaintances. By keeping busy, I do not have to examine if I am happy and have meaning in my life. I definitely feel guilty unless someone else has volunteered. I double- or triple-book myself, rationalizing that I can take a conference call in the car while driving child number one and number two to their respective activities. Then I can drop off the dog at the veterinarian while taking conference call number two with child number three in the car for her activities. All the while, I can check my Blackberry for any messages, because isn't modern technology so wonderful! And yes, I catch myself trying to keep up with others for fear that I may miss out on a career-enabling move if I do not do more, be more, and commit to more than others. Is it any wonder I think I am a superhero?

Help Is on the Way!

Recall the story of Sandi. Here is how she unraveled the Superwoman Trap and released herself from its bonds:

>> Sandi expanded on her new, more realistic expectations. By clarifying her criteria of what mattered most to her, she was then able to prioritize what she focused her attention on. As a result, when opportunities or requests came her way, she was able to agree quickly to those that were in alignment with her success criteria. Having this clarity of what was important allowed her then to decline activities or tasks that did not move her toward her goals. She had cut back on her work hours, learned to say "No" at work, and scaled back her community volunteer work to a more manageable level. As a result, she was able to spend more time with her family or on herself, rather than with groups of strangers at community events.

As I exclaimed, "Oh, my gosh," and then projected my fears onto her situation, I asked about her career. Would her career suffer if she worked in moderation or said "No" occasionally? Sandi quickly responded, "Not at all!" She no longer had that concern as she searched long and hard to determine what success meant to her. Her contemplation revealed that what mattered to her was more than just climbing the corporate ladder; she had reframed it to focus on the reasons she enjoyed her work. These included having fulfilling work, feeling she was making a difference at work, having a good team or colleagues to work with, and being able to leave work with enough energy to enjoy her life, her family, and her friends. As a result, she now had a renewed sense of peace and confidence for herself despite her continuing career aspirations and the multiple demands placed on her. <<

The "Fantastic Four"

Being busy when you are enjoying yourself, doing what you want to be doing, and feeling like you are hitting your stride or are in your element is an amazing experience. Everything clicks and you feel the synergy of those around you. However, it is no longer fun when that pace and need to take on more gets to the point that you need superhuman powers to accomplish everything you expect from yourself. So, if you recognize yourself in that description (and you know you do), try these four fantastic ways to avoid the Superwoman Trap:

1. Shed the superhero costume: Okay, it's time to take off the superhero costume and have a look inside at the real you, not the facade you have been putting on for all to see. You must decide what is most important to you. Clarifying what matters most is required to determine what gets done versus what would be nice to do but not essential. Taking the time to do this provides clarity about what you focus your attention on each day. Yes, this is a scary and daunting task, and it takes courage to stand in front of the mirror and shed that protective costume that you are so used to wearing and have a good long look at who you are today. Not who you think you need to be, or who you used to be, or who you would like to become—reflect on who you are today.

This may seem an arduous and overwhelming task, but it is possible if you break it down into these easy steps. First, make a list of the characteristics you believe define you—the characteristics you value for yourself and want others to describe about you. When you have fully itemized your list of characteristics, make another list of what those characteristics would look like in day-to-day life. For example, if you wrote, "being family-oriented," you might list "spend time playing with kids" as your measurable day-to-day contribution to being the person you are today and always wanted to be. This extraordinarily useful but also profoundly uncomfortable process is necessary for you to move from the Superwoman Trap to a more balanced positive state.

2. Face your fears and guilt: Each time you find yourself asked to take on one more task, stop and ask yourself: "What is driving me? Do I feel I have to be busy? Am I afraid of being left out? Do I feel guilty unless I agree to all demands at work and home? Do I feel I only exist as a reflection in other people's eyes? Do I desire to please everyone at the expense of myself? Do I keep busy to avoid looking inward?"

Deep inside, you know you cannot accept every invitation, agree to every volunteer request, donate your time, money, talent, or all of the above, to every cause you are asked to without serious consequences to yourself. Yet you still feel guilty for saying "No." Not anymore! Every time life brings you to a decision point, remind yourself that you had the courage to examine your fears and they have no place in your life. You are no longer scared to make a mistake in case someone notices and criticizes you. Pull out your list of what defines you and how you contribute regularly. With that in mind, evaluate the request and go toward the choice that allows you to live out your values instead of feeding into your fears. It can be that simple! Your days of fear-based, guilt-ridden decision making are over now that you have faced your fears and guilt. You are your own master not a superhero!

3. Give yourself a break: As the pace of your daily life increases, remember to find time to give yourself a break. Your highly organized plans may begin to crumble under the pressure as more demands are put on your time and energy. Accepting that you may not be able to do things as thoroughly as you prefer can be like giving yourself a break. One technique I find especially useful in enabling this is "abundance thinking."

The superhero is concerned for survival in a world of scarcity—a world that is relying on your unique superhero powers, as no one else can do what you can do. As you have shed your superhero costume, reframe your thoughts to those of abundance. You will be better able to give yourself a break if you believe that there will always be enough people, enough things, or enough money to handle the work that needs to be done. Rosamund and Benjamin Zander, in their book *The Art of Possibility,* write that when you are oriented to abundance, you care less about being in control, you take more risks, you dream bigger, and most importantly, you set the context of your life and let it unfold. So, in times when you have that urge to haul out the superhero costume, think abundance and give yourself a break— you are not the only one responsible for justice and humanitarian service in the world.

4. Surround yourself with positive: Never underestimate the power of positive thinking and surrounding yourself with people who focus on the possibilities. Now, this does not mean we all have to become Pollyannas or "happy, happy" all the time. It is more an adjustment in perspective or reframing of how you look at your world. It is as simple as the advice I was given when I learned to snow ski through trees: The key is to focus on the spaces between the trees, *not* the trees. In skiing, as in life, it is about focusing on those spaces or possibilities, not the obstacles or problems. Ask a special friend or co-worker to be your sounding board when you feel as if you are being overloaded. Be with people who can share your anxieties and then remind you of the options that are available, not the limitations that might never materialize. Remember, even the real superheroes have a supporting cast of characters, including friends, co-workers, butlers, and/or love interests!

Letting Go of the Superhero

That day in the car with my son was truly an "aha" moment for me. Since that awakening, I have learned that the Superwoman Trap is *not* inevitable. Rather, through examining our fears and defining who we are, we have the ability to make the choices that move us forward, away from the Superwoman Trap and toward the wonderful and powerful people we already are. So when faced with the challenge to take on too much, resist the shiny cape and matching turbo boots—no super-heroes required!

Anne Baldwin

Anne Baldwin is an experienced consultant, facilitator, and speaker who specializes in leadership, change management, generational diversity, and specialized health care content.

Her passion and energy for life is clearly evident in her humorous, informative, and perceptive message. During her presentations, Anne's enthusiasm energizes and motivates her participants. The combination of her true-to-life anecdotes and down-to-earth approach resonates with her audience and provides real learning.

Anne's education includes a Bachelor and Masters of Science in Nursing. When she is not getting her passionate message out, Anne can most often be seen riding her bike everywhere with her three children and husband in tow.

Business Name: One Step Consulting
Address: 4279 Hobson Road, Kelowna, BC V1W 1Y4
Telephone: 250-764-0927
Email: abaldwin64@shaw.ca
Speaking Affiliations: Canadian Association of Professional Speakers,
                    Vancouver Chapter (Professional Membership)

Favorite Quotation:
Let the world know you as you are, not as you think you should be, because sooner or later, if you are posing, you will forget the pose, and then where are you?

Fanny Brice

Arlene Jorgenson

HEALTHSERV Saskatchewan Limited

How to Stay Cool When Your Pants Are on Fire

» In the early 1990s, as an occupational health nurse for the federal government in Manitoba, the most frequently requested workshop I presented was on the subject of stress management. At that time "stress" and "burnout" were new-fashioned words. Faithfully—and I would like to think, skillfully—I presented interactive, fun-filled workshops for workers. My belief was that my courses would change their lives, and help them cope better with the ever-mounting stresses of downsizing, restructuring, layoffs, and cutbacks.

Enthusiastically, I taught techniques such as deep breathing and visualization, which the thinking of the time promised would aid weary and overwrought souls to find peace and balance amidst the turmoil of their work lives. ("In through your nose…and out through your mouth…in through your nose…"). At the same time, a book by Dr. Peter Hanson, *The Joy of Stress*, was flying off the shelves with its practical theories on building up our resistance to stress with enough sleep, good food, and respecting that we need time to recover, in body and soul, from stressful events. All of these ideas were great, but somehow my sense was that something was missing. It became clear to me that successful stress management had to be more than a series of techniques. «

Getting Older and Better

Life has a way of taking the shiny edge off our naïveté. In this new millennium, I find myself older and much more sober about the realities of the struggle with the inevitable ebb and flow of living. With this comes the realization that "the grip" on life needs to be lighter, not tighter. There is no point in getting older and worse, so how about embracing the quest of getting older and better.

Teaching people how to keep their pants from catching fire in the first place seemed to make more sense than teaching them to put out the fire. As a professional speaker, I wondered if the topic would be a "hot seller" (pardon the bad pun)! It is sound occupational health practice to prevent the accident in the first place. My sense was that this would be as successful as signing me up for the latest fad diet—nice idea on paper, but on closer inspection anyone could see that I was not likely to be victorious!

As human beings, we have lots of good intentions. But, in our hurry-scurry world, when heads are down, and noses are to the grindstone, what we really need is to be reminded of the basics. We need to create the mindset that will bring us back to our true values. To help with this, the following is a summary of my ABCs for "keeping cool when your pants are on fire."

A—A Is for Attitude

» "Come and play Barbies, Auntie Arlene," invited my five-year-old niece, Hanna, from the living room, where she and her older brother were playing. I made an excuse about needing to finish cleaning up in the kitchen first. "Come on, just sit down and play Barbies with us, Auntie," she pleaded again. Finally, I relented and joined them on the floor with the pile of Barbie clothes and dolls. I wasn't excited about it, because I really didn't know how to play Barbies. I was the oldest child from a hard-working farm family. I don't remember playing Barbies; I just remember working!

So, I looked at the pile of Barbie dolls and clothes, and thought what my first move should be. One option would be to observe the other participants and model their behavior. A few questions of inquiry might help: Is there an objective? Is there a destination? Is there dialogue? "Oh, Auntie Arlene, you just play Barbies!" Hanna instructed.

Apparently, the only purpose of playing Barbies is to put their clothes on and take them off. When you have mixed and matched a good outfit, and found shoes to go with it, you hold your Barbie up and show everyone how nice she looks. Then, you rip off the clothes and start hunting for another ensemble. You also have to help Ken, because Ken has trouble finding enough outfits! I was feeling quite pleased with myself, mixing, matching, showing, helping Ken, when all of a sudden, my five-going-on-25-year-old niece said, "Oh, Auntie Arlene, that doesn't match!" How soon they learn there is a way to make it more complicated! **«**

The objective was to have fun! Do you remember when your parents said, "We will support you, whatever path you choose in life, as long as you're having fun and enjoying what you're doing"? We've forgotten that! Lives are now complicated, over-scheduled, and way too serious! Don't get me wrong, you should take your work seriously, yet it is dangerous to take *yourself* too seriously. It kills joy, spontaneity, and fun. Has anyone said to you lately, "You're no fun anymore?" Ouch! Maybe, it's time to adjust attitudes a bit, and start to lighten up, loosen up, and be goofier. Become more acquainted with fun, play, and recreation, and you will reconnect with the joy of living.

Exercise

What are the things that make you smile, laugh, and bring you joy? Make a list in the space below:

_____

_____

_____

_____

_____

_____

Now, make a point of doing those things more often. Plan them into your schedule, and guard them as closely as you guard your obligations to those significant people in your life. You would never think of letting down your loved ones, so don't shortchange yourself. This responsibility is to your own wellness!

B—Fix Your Brakes, Not Your Accelerator

If you know what your destination is, then it's easy to say "No" to the things that won't get you there.

» After working for five years as a community health nurse in Northern Saskatchewan and in the Northwest Territories, I found myself packing for Winnipeg, Manitoba the day after Christmas in 1985. My (then) husband, a pilot, had received an attractive job offer to fly with the corporate fleet of a large company. Moving "south" was the goal of most government people up north, so I should have been happy. My qualifications as a nurse allowed me to transfer with the government and start work immediately in an occupational health position.

Five years later, I was back in Saskatoon—with another transfer and a promotion and supervising staff—with the determination to get my life back on track after leaving my abusive husband. In my frenzy to prove myself, I often worked late, took work home, and regularly overscheduled myself, resulting in the stress of being late or missing appointments. "Yes" was my response to every request as I was desperate to be liked. I took my job and myself very seriously. My degrees and certificates were lined up on the wall behind my desk, hoping to prove my excellence as a nurse and a human being.

Consequently, I ended up being exactly like many of the workers who came to see me through the Employee Assistance Program: suffering from the physical and emotional symptoms of ill health that we often lump together in the non-specific term of burnout. «

These symptoms—including daily headaches, weight gain, food binges, and waking up exhausted no matter how much I slept—had come on so gradually, and had become so routine, that I accepted them as "normal." The dark circles under my eyes were attributed to my fair coloring. Putting up with regular skin breakouts and rashes, I believed it was just hormones. My busyness kept me from attending family gatherings and babysitting my new nephews. As a "smart nurse," I was sure all I needed was a weekend of sleep, and everything would be fine! My counselor finally got me to agree that I was not well, and that it was okay to take some time off, not knowing that it would be three months before I would be completely well!

There is no shame in getting to the end of your rope and feeling as if you are completely losing it. But, for goodness sake, tie a knot in the end of that rope so that whenever you get close to it again, you will feel it, and not let yourself go any further. While still working hard at my career, the top item on my goal sheet for each year is now "Prevent Burnout—Continuous Renewal." Burnout has not sabotaged me again.

As modern people, we aspire to have anything we want.
But NOT ALL AT THE SAME TIME!
Fix your brakes, not your accelerator.

The following are some great ideas—many that people have shared in my seminars—to help learn how to fix your brakes.

Top 10 Ways to Fix Your Brakes

1. **Turn it off!** We turn off our answering machine and Blackberry before going on vacation. Who needs to come home to two weeks of messages that are too old or too late, and feel guilty?
2. **Leave it!** Leave work at work; keep it from spilling over into your home time.
3. **Unplug it!** Leave your phone unplugged during the supper hour. Family time is too valuable to allow interruptions. Remember that families that play together stay together.
4. **Turn it down!** Choose time to turn off the radio in your vehicle. Value the quiet time to think instead.

5. **De-clutter!** Use the "one-year" rule: anything that hasn't been used or worn in the past year needs to be tossed, sold, recycled, or given away.

6. **Use technology carefully**. Be choosy—only my office and my husband have the number for my cell phone. Stop being available all the time.

7. **Match your goals with your desired workload.** Make choices that support your health. We have always dreamed of a cabin at the lake but realized we could rent many, many times before it would be worth the cost, headache, and overwork to buy one.

8. **Banish perfectionist ideals.** Watch for this in both your work and personal life. You may tidy up for company at home, yet five minutes after they arrive, no one notices! Know they came for the hospitality, not to inspect your house cleaning.

9. **Just say "No"!** Avoid giving excuses when declining a request. Say, "Thank you, but no, I/we aren't going to participate this year." Then drop it!

10. **Think twice—leap once.** Make great choices about how you use your time and energy. Know it can take years to get off those committees that it took five minutes to sign up for!

C—Commit to Being an Encourager

It's a no-brainer to be a complainer. But, it takes some thought to give praise and thanks where you ought.

When marrying my "new" wonderful husband, Stu, it was a package deal. He brought with him adult children, their spouses, and a lovely assortment of grandchildren. Not having children myself, this leap into grandma-hood was quite startling!

» One day, my grandson, Shaun, called me on the phone. He was about two and a half at the time. I didn't know it was him at first, because he couldn't really talk yet. All I could just hear this little breathing, with his mom in the background, encouraging him, "Tell Grandma what you did." With me encouraging him with my "grandma voice" from my end of the phone, and his mom encouraging him from the other, he finally told me what he had called to tell me he had done. "POOP!" Well!

Because I'm his grandma, I knew exactly what this meant: Shaun was successful on the potty! He loved the cheering and applause he received from me while telling him what a big boy he was. Then I called Grandpa, so he could hear the important news first-hand! **«**

With little kids, the connection between encouragement and building up self-esteem is understood. This, in turn, builds up self-confidence, which in turn, gives them a solid foundation for a successful life. To show this, you give them tangibles such as stickers and stars, put their artwork on the fridge, attend every piano recital and hockey game while cheering and videotaping it. With being an adult comes the realization that there are fewer stickers and stars. It reminds me of an experience with a government job at annual performance review time. The bottom line was that, *Once a year I will tell you if I like you. For the rest of the time if I change my mind, I will let you know!*

As an occupational health nurse, I've studied and experienced first-hand what motivates people in the workplace, and it always points to the same thing: workers rank "appreciation" as most important to them. People crave being appreciated! (By the way, number two is "feeling in on things"; number three is "an understanding attitude"; number four is "job security"; and number five is "fair wages." A poster of this top-10 list can be printed from my website: www.arlenejorgenson.com.)

» When starting HEALTHSERV in 1992, and acquiring staff as we grew, I worried that my employees might not be motivated or happy, as I could not pay top wages. I soon learned that they were motivated and would stay or leave based on more important values than money. As a result, I created a workplace where people were appreciated, had a sense of belonging, and felt that they were part of the bigger picture. **«**

Commit to being an "encourager" in order to meet that most basic of needs in people: the need to be appreciated. The following two ideas—"Encouragement Mail" and an "Encouragement File"—will help.

Encouragement Mail

» While sitting in my bank manager's office one day awaiting her return, I looked at her bulletin board. These handy office fixtures can tell us so much! Bulletin boards are the occupational health nurse's method of taking the blood pressure of an organization—they give clues about the values, beliefs, and activities of that workplace. On her bulletin board, there were little green notes with a cartoon fellow holding up his thumb and the slogan, "You made the difference." When she returned, I asked about those notes. "Oh, those are encouragement notes from co-workers. With everyone working flex-time, part-time, and Saturdays, it's so hard to get everyone together for a meeting or a celebration, so our manager instituted the idea of encouragement notes. When we catch someone doing something well, we send a note of encouragement."

"You really all do this?" I remarked, almost not believing something so simple would be happening in this stiff corporate world. "Oh, yes! Some people do it more and some people less. Our manager spends the first 20 minutes of each day writing out encouragement notes from the day before." Contemplating the effect this idea would have on workplace morale, excitement grew in me. Still curious, I asked, "What are the round pink notes?" "Oh," her eyes twinkling and her voice lowering as she answered, "those are from the boss!" «

Wow! Imagine what you would do if you came into your office in the morning and you found a round pink note on your desk. You knew it would be something positive from your supervisor. Would you hang up your coat, check your email, put your lunch in the fridge, get a cup of coffee, and check the lottery numbers from yesterday first? I don't think so! You would rip that little note open, and savor it—then, maybe post it on your bulletin board!

Since that memorable event at my bank, I've shared this idea with workplaces and groups all over who are struggling with the same issues of morale, team spirit, and staying connected. The result is my extensive collection of "Corporate Encouragement Mail" ideas from all types of workplaces. Here are some of the best:

- A nursing home copied ghost shapes during the Halloween season with the phrase, "You did a boooo-tiful job" written across the front for staff, volunteers, and family to use.
- One government office printed up little cards that said, "You Done Good" for everyone to use. Since they handle very tough and draining cases, it was hard for staff to stay cheerful. Several months later, I saw the manager at a conference and asked how the Encouragement Mail idea was going. "Oh," she said, "one of the sourpusses was quick to point out that our slogan was bad grammar. But, that same person has all her little cards she's received lined up across the front of her desk."
- With volunteers, remember that your Encouragement Mail, such as a sincere, written thank you, is all they get!
- A hospital was proud to show me their "Tree of Thanks." It was originally assembled in the dining room during the Thanksgiving season so staff, family, and volunteers could write notes of thanks on colored leaves to fill up the tree. Eventually, it had been "transplanted" into the staff room but the notes continued across the wall, onto the ceiling, and around one corner. It was explained that this was done as the tree had become "too precious to throw in the garbage, so we just keep adding to it."

Life is short—never miss an opportunity to send a lovely handwritten note in the mail expressing your praise and delight at an accomplishment, promotion, picture in the paper, nomination, or award. In our busy electronic world, the sentiment of a written note will stand out and be cherished. It is mind-boggling how many times I've sent someone a note to say "Good for you!" and they've responded that it was the only one they had received.

Encouragement File

If you really do reap what you sow, you will end up with lots of your own "E-Mail." Where will you keep it all? Here is an idea! Put all of your Encouragement Mail into a special folder. (Some of you may be already using a shoebox—which would make it an "E-Box"!) My folder is labeled "Arlene's Encouragement File," and it is full of all kinds of lovely stuff: thank-you notes, congratulation letters, cards from flowers, jokes sent to me, news clippings that mention me or my business, and pictures that my grandkids have drawn for me.

Now, on a good day, I don't need to look in there. But on a bad day, when I am feeling like the schmuck of the earth and nothing is turning out right, I close the door and go through my "E-Files." Those encouraging notes—and the praise and compliments that were sincerely written to me—are the truth about who I am! They counteract the doldrums. Human nature is such that it is much easier to collect negative messages and replay them in our minds than to remember the good ones. An "E-File" is essential to help keep perspective, especially when feeling challenged.

For those of you with children, or who work with youth, teaching them to have a file like this is a must. The world is very quick to point out to young people that they are not tall enough, shapely enough, slim enough, cute enough, smart enough, popular enough, and on, and on, and on. It's not right.

Final Words From an Encourager

You've just read about this nurse's ABCs for "keeping cool when your pants are on fire."

Know that checking your *attitude* daily helps you to be aware of gripping life more lightly, not more tightly. It makes you more fun to be around, and you'll live longer. Wouldn't you rather have lines from laughing than from worrying?

Fix your *brakes*, not your accelerator. It's easier on your "engine," and you'll enjoy the scenery much more.

Commit yourself to being an Encourager—for others and for yourself. Start by adopting one easy idea that will feed others' basic need to be appreciated, and one idea to help you keep up your own morale.

Through these ABCs, my intent has been to inspire you to make an even stronger commitment to your own health and wellness, so that you are truly enjoying the time of your life. Remember to:

Stay cool when your pants are on fire!

Arlene A. Jorgenson

Arlene A. Jorgenson has been an adult educator, and award-winning speaker and trainer for over 20 years, delighting North American audiences with her practical wisdom and her own brand of humor.

With a degree in nursing and a specialty designation in occupational health nursing, Arlene founded HEALTHSERV in 1992 as an occupational health consulting company serving the safety and health needs of industry in Western Canada. HEALTHSERV's specialties are substance abuse testing, policy development and pre-employment medical testing. Arlene's business acumen has led to her winning a 2003 NSBA Innovation Award, 2006 Healthcare Excellence Award, and most recently, 2007 ABEX Service Industry Award.

Arlene's speaking focuses on worker appreciation, and personal and organizational success, and she particularly enjoys presenting opening and closing keynotes. Her signature stories and side-splitting humor leave the audience recalling her messages years later. Now that's a testimonial!

Arlene was previously published in *Expert Women Who Speak, Speak Out! Volume 2*. She has several keynotes available on tape and CD, and through her website.

Business Name: A. Jorgenson & Associates Consulting Inc.

Address: 2228 Avenue C North, Saskatoon, SK S7L 6C4

Telephone: 306-374-9079

Email: ajorgenson@healthservsask.com

Web Addresses: www.arlenejorgenson.com

www.healthservsask.com

Professional Memberships: Canadian Association of Professional Speakers, Canadian Society of Safety Engineering, Women Entrepreneurs of Saskatchewan, Canadian Occupational Health Nurses Organization

Favorite Saying:
Life is for living, loving and laughing…not for worrying, whining and wallowing!

To accomplish great things, we must not only act, but also dream; not only plan, but also believe.

Anatole France

Shona Welsh

Momentum Learning Inc.

The 10 Laws of Leadership Resilience

In today's world, most leadership positions involve being a change agent, and that often comes with tension, resentment, and worry. A leader's ability not only to survive but to thrive rests heavily on resilience. Leadership can be very lonely because people don't necessarily share your vision—at least not at first. But just because you're outnumbered doesn't mean you're wrong. John F. Kennedy was outnumbered by those who didn't believe the United States would put a man on the moon by the end of the 1960s.

As defined in the *Penguin Pocket English Dictionary*, resilience is the "ability to recover from or adjust to misfortune or change." Research shows that an inability to do those things is among the key reasons for leadership failure. It's not because leaders are unintelligent, but because they don't know where to start.

The most formidable leadership challenge I've ever faced was in establishing leadership development at an international engineering firm. Being charged with implementing cultural change within the organization was a daunting task, and living the 10 Laws of Leadership Resilience served me well in fulfilling this mandate. Focusing on and returning to these laws when I felt challenged was the foundation for keeping my equilibrium, optimism, and vision. These 10 laws form a strong foundation for any leader:

1. You can only change yourself;
2. Notice where you exist;
3. Beware of "frozen judgments";

4. Embrace your dark side;

5. Commit to transparency;

6. Develop and maintain self-reflection;

7. Never compromise your integrity;

8. You don't need to have all the answers;

9. Pick the right hills to die on;

10. Never be afraid to make a decision.

Law #1: You Can Only Change Yourself

We've all heard some version of this principle, but *knowing it* and *living it* are two different things.

> » During my first year at the engineering firm, my most confounding lesson was that even though they had hired me to implement change, had committed resources, and had publicly announced it, it didn't mean they were serious.
>
> After a year of banging my head against corporate walls, all I had was a headache. Anxious to avert a career concussion, I made an inner decision that transformed my perspective. But it wasn't a great leadership epiphany. I had merely rediscovered a favorite quote from Mahatma Gandhi: "You must be the change you wish to see in the world."
>
> If I wanted to see change in the organization, I had to model it. So I stopped banging my head against their walls and created my own doors. I changed the way I communicated to suit the engineering world. I changed the way I dealt with people who tried to intimidate me. I changed the focus of my department to reflect broader business goals. The organization didn't do anything. Not until I changed myself first.
>
> When I left six years later, one executive said, "What will we do without you? You've become the conscience of the company." «

Resilient leaders know that lasting change starts from within. If you want your organization to reflect your leadership goals and vision, start with yourself. What can *you* do that will inspire a reality different from the present? The next nine laws form a roadmap that leads you to that reality.

Law #2: Notice Where You Exist

» One colleague made it abundantly clear that not only was he was suffering my existence, he would sabotage my efforts.

Both a brilliant engineer and a gifted businessman, he was president of one our most successful companies. He had a lot of power. For months, I obsessed about "converting" him. I worked endless hours anticipating his objections. I drove myself crazy countering his political moves. I had silent anxiety attacks in his presence.

Eventually, I realized my growing negativity about the company was vested in him. I had been focusing the majority of my time, energy, and thoughts on him. That's where I existed. And it had blinded me to success opportunities. «

One of the greatest services you can do for yourself is notice where you exist in your mind. Where do you focus? Do you constantly relive the day one of your managers insulted you, or do you focus on his later apology? Do you focus on people and things that will help you leverage success?

» Once I realized I existed in the president's negative world, it compelled me to seek out more positive real estate. Many colleagues were willing to give me a chance. So I moved mental locales to be with them. My perspective and energy reversed inside a month, and I regrouped to establish some highly successful programs.

The real measure of success came two years later. As I gave a presentation, several presidents added their learning success stories. At the conclusion, the negative president looked accusingly at me, saying, "Why don't I ever get to do anything like that?" It was clear he didn't like where he existed any longer. «

Resilient leaders examine where they exist to assess if it's serving them well or it needs to change.

Law #3: Beware of "Frozen Judgments"

Have you ever encountered someone who continues to believe you're the same person you were years ago? One supervisor from 20 years ago continues to believe that I have trouble dealing with detail work. In fact, I have developed a number of skills to help me deal more effectively with that challenge. In this case, I am the target of a "frozen judgment"—the assumption that I have remained the same, with no credit given for growth and maturity.

To keep up with the frantic pace of our lives, we often rush to simplify complex relationships by applying frozen judgments. But we forget that people are always works in progress. It may be easier for us, but it does a disservice to them.

» One colleague was a toxic individual who deflated everyone around him. Though a gifted engineer, his abrasiveness meant we were constantly recruiting to replace his team members. His boss was either unwilling or unable to take action. Finally, a new supervisor fired him.

Fast forward several years. While conducting a mentoring workshop for a client, the troublesome engineer showed up as a participant. I couldn't imagine why my client had selected him as a mentor.

When he arrived, his warm greeting delighted me. Unable to adjust my thinking, though, I prepared myself for a tough day. But not only was he enthusiastic and positive, he made great suggestions and repeatedly helped others. I was astounded.

At one point, he spoke to me about his time at our former company. I gained significant insight into some failures of leadership that predated my arrival, many of which were responsible for his toxic behavior. While I believe we all choose our attitude in any situation, I couldn't help but feel for the hopeless context in which he perceived himself. He acknowledged that being fired was the best thing that happened to him; it freed him to re-engage positively in another company. «

I realized I had applied my own frozen judgments to this engineer. I hadn't given him any credit for the ability to reflect on his past experience and learn from it. Given what he told me, coupled with his behavior during the workshop, I completely reframed my view of him.

I've observed that many leaders typecast employees, believing their current responsibilities and behaviors are all they're capable of or willing to do. A resilient leader must be willing to assess and re-assess continuously the impressions they hold about employees. Frozen judgments might make it easier to make decisions but could also lead to overlooking immense talent and potential right under your nose. And that makes the job of a leader more—not less—stressful.

Law #4: Embrace Your Dark Side

Modern leadership is complex and leaders must be able to navigate the minefield of organizational politics. This can create much frustration and tension that can easily morph into resentment and anger. Everyone has negative and uncharitable thoughts from time to time. These thoughts are silent saboteurs that, unless exposed to daylight, can lead to being a judgmental person who exists in and works from a negative place.

The first thing to do is accept your dark side. You are certainly not alone in petty and vindictive thoughts. No matter how good a leader you are, how considerate you try to be, how well you get along with others, you will occasionally think and feel these things. You're human.

Next, you need to find someone you trust outside your organization and on whose confidentiality you can depend. Because leadership is a very lonely job, there is no one at work with whom this would be appropriate. Your confidante should be someone who knows you for the good person you are, and with whom you will feel safe to bare all your darkest thoughts about situations and people with whom you are struggling.

> » A colleague of mine and I spend hours bouncing ideas around and generally venting about employees and clients. When either of us has had a bad day, we allow 15 minutes at the beginning of conversations for venting. The rule is we must get every horrible, mean-spirited, uncharitable thought and feeling out on the table during that time. Once time is up, we do one of two things: 1) Think of everything that's good about the person or the situation, or 2) Move into solution-focused problem solving.

What we've discovered is that the process of venting frees our mental energy to focus on positives. We don't hold lingering resentment, and nothing festers to become full-out verbal brawls at work. We can engage in positive, respectful communications.

Contrast this to when I used to keep everything stuffed inside, not wanting to admit my insidious thoughts. It would build up to an explosion, at which point I would use anger as my tool. But it was as much anger directed at myself for being petty as it was anger toward others. **«**

Resilient leaders look in the mirror and admit their petty thoughts. They accept them and find optimal ways and means to move through and beyond them.

Law #5: Commit to Transparency

My son taught me about transparency. Ever since he could talk, he's asked me to explain my reasoning behind things. He has never let me get away with the old parent standby, "Because I said so." He doesn't always like or agree with my reasoning, but he respects and appreciates the honesty with which it is delivered. No one, not even a child, likes to be told "No" without having a clear understanding of the reasons behind it.

Leadership is no different. Employees don't have to like or agree with your decisions, but if you commit to being completely transparent in your thinking, they usually respect and accept it. For example, I often ask employees in my workshops if they agree with and/or like every decision their leaders make. Almost everyone says "No," but they still work there. Most indicate that they've stayed because not only are decisions explained to them, they've also had an opportunity to be heard. In other words, not only do their leaders make their own thinking transparent, they openly listen to and consider everyone else's thinking.

» After five years of being a successful change agent, I began looking for another challenge. I noticed our organization had poor public relations and I had had a previous career in that field.

So I approached the CEO and pitched the idea of adding public relations to my responsibilities. He was receptive. I spent three months benchmarking other companies and developing a viable business plan.

Several times, he had questions. Each time, I responded promptly. Six months later, I still hadn't received a decision. Finally, he confessed he hadn't read anything I'd sent. His continual questions only feigned interest. It turns out he knew I was looking for a new challenge and was afraid that if he didn't provide it, I would leave. At the same time, he was completely bamboozled by the notion of public relations and I might as well have been speaking gibberish.

I didn't know either of those things until months later. Consequently, I left our meeting feeling angry, humiliated, and completely disrespected. Would I have liked it if he'd turned me down at the beginning? No. But it would have saved a lot of time, effort, and misplaced excitement at the prospect of a new challenge. And I would have maintained my respect and regard for him, never mind my trust. **«**

We're often afraid to be transparent with our employees—afraid they'll be annoyed with us, afraid they'll lose respect for us, afraid we'll lose them. And yet, if we aren't transparent, many of the things we fear will actually happen. I *was* annoyed. I *did* lose respect. And I left soon after that.

Resilient leaders tell the truth and tell it early. Make your thinking completely transparent. How did you get from A to Z? What were all the steps in between? It may seem counterintuitive, but the more transparent you are about yourself and your thinking, the more you'll gain trust and respect—even if it's bad news.

Law #6: Develop and Maintain Self-Reflection

Most of the 10 Laws of Leadership Resilience involve some form of self-reflection. Your ongoing and primary job as a leader is to reflect on your own behavior and motivations so you can show up as the leader you want to be, while attending to the goals and bottom line of your organization. Additionally, you need to encourage and support the same kind of self-reflection in those you lead. In other words, you want to build as much self-reflection and, ultimately, resilience in your employees as you do in yourself.

>> One colleague was very well intentioned, but his behavior often had an unintended impact on employees. Worse, he was oblivious to it.

It was clear that he was genuinely confused and concerned about his employees' lack of faith in him, so after we'd built a good working relationship, I began dropping by his office regularly. Mostly, I asked him questions and he talked. He didn't realize I was coaching him to self-reflect, to analyze the impact of his behavior. It got to the point that, when he saw me standing in his doorway, he would hang his head and jokingly say, "What have I done now?" «

If Law #1 (you can only change yourself) is the foundation of leadership resilience, then self-reflection is the cornerstone. To paraphrase Henry Ford, "If you don't know where you're going, any place will do" (www.quotegarden.com).

Resilient leaders ask themselves about their role in any given situation. They ask such questions as, "How have I contributed?" "How have I not contributed?" "If I put myself in my employees' shoes, how would I feel? What would I think?" Unless and until you do this, and require your employees to do the same, there's a good chance you'll end up somewhere you don't want to be.

Law #7: Never Compromise Your Integrity

A non-negotiable tenet of resilient leadership is personal integrity. According to self-esteem expert Nathaniel Branden, in *The Six Pillars of Self-Esteem*, integrity is "the reputation we acquire with ourselves." If we compromise our fundamental values, we lose our leadership guidance system, the thing that keeps us focused and sane when those around us are insisting on "minor" changes and deviations. (Recall the faulty o-rings on the space shuttle *Challenger* that were dismissed as "minor deviations.")

>> For years, I fought a tough battle in my organization to build a culture that valued learning. So I was really excited when one usually resistant president became interested in running workshops about values.

Unfortunately, disaster struck two weeks before our first session when massive layoffs were announced. It was particularly tough because they were still recovering from previous layoffs. In this challenging context, I concluded our values workshops would be postponed.

When the president phoned to discuss workshop arrangements, I balked. I explained that doing a values workshop in the midst of layoffs would be willfully destructive. He simply pressed harder. As he became more agitated, I calmly kept repeating myself. One of the company's values was being "family-oriented and caring" and no one was feeling that way.

His reaction escalated to screaming obscenities at me before severing the call. Given his position and power, I went home and told my husband we should get used to having toast for dinner, as I was sure the CEO would fire me the next day. **«**

Honoring your integrity means that you must be willing to be fired every day for doing the right thing. Although it seems counterintuitive, standing up for your values rarely results in firing. Even better, knowing you'll survive with your values intact builds one more layer of resilience.

By the way, when that president finally called me back, he was charming and pleasant. It seems he'd decided it wasn't a good time to do the values workshops. And I never heard a word about it from the CEO.

Law #8: You Don't Need to Have All the Answers

It's remarkable how much we know at 20 and how little at 40. Experience generally teaches us that most things exist in a million shades of grey. Leadership is no different.

» One year, another of our companies was facing hard times due to losing a large client. The president was preparing for an all-employee meeting and was extremely stressed.

After talking with him at length, I realized his stress wasn't so much about the tough announcement. It was that he didn't know what the future held, didn't have a plan, and didn't know where to start. He asked for advice on what to say.

"Say you don't know," I replied. He was dumbfounded.

"I can't say that!" he responded vehemently.

"Why not?" I said.

"Because I'm the president! I'm supposed to show them the way out of this!"

"What do you think would happen if you said you didn't know?" I responded.

"They'd lose respect. They'd think I didn't deserve to be their leader."

"If you go out there and invent stuff you're not sure of, and then can't make it happen, they'll lose respect anyway," I said. "What have you got to lose?"

So he tossed his notes and delivered a heartfelt plea. He told the audience about the lost client, that he didn't know where to go, and he was open to anyone's ideas.

The support overwhelmed him. He was swamped for weeks with eager employees pitching great solutions. In the end, the company not only weathered the storm but developed new markets. **«**

Later, he told me it was a turning point in his career. He had never once considered admitting ignorance, believing leaders should always appear knowledgeable and confident. While that's certainly true to a point, he learned a valuable lesson about inspiring employees. And his leadership resilience probably increased because he'd done the unthinkable—and survived.

Law #9: Pick the Right Hills to Die On

A key responsibility of leadership is assessing which situations are worth battling over and which just aren't worth the time, aggravation, and potential resistance. In military terms, this means picking the hills on which you're going to launch a full-out assault, knowing there will be some casualties, and ignoring hills not worth climbing, much less conquering.

» In one organization in which I worked, leaders had to decide if the personal use of company vehicles was a hill to die on. Employees regularly took company vehicles home and were allowed to use them for simple errands, such as grocery shopping or visiting a friend. Everyone knew that taking vehicles on camping trips across the country or even to the nearest city for a weekend getaway was not allowed, even though there was no formal policy. Unfortunately, one person flagrantly disregarded the practice and got into an accident several thousand miles away.

At first, certain leaders wanted to ban all personal use of company vehicles for any reason. But when they experienced the backlash from the high percentage of employees who had been consistently trustworthy and responsible, they relented and decided to deal only with the offending individual. In other words, it wasn't a hill to die on, considering the cost in employee goodwill and engagement. **«**

Deciding which issues are hills to die on isn't always easy. No matter what you do, there will be critics. Resilient leaders accept that they can't please everyone all the time and skillfully assess their employees' reactions: Who is opposed? Who is in favor? Who is neutral and therefore open to new information? What's possible to achieve today and what needs to be left for another day, or just simply left? What will it cost us (financially and otherwise) to conquer this hill and is it worth it?

Law #10: Never Be Afraid to Make a Decision

» After much observation, I concluded that our leaders struggled with tough decisions about employees. To relieve themselves of responsibility, they would do one of two things:

1. If they liked you but declined to continue your initiative, they would shuffle you around various companies doing indeterminate, non-challenging jobs. As long as you didn't bother them, they were happy to keep paying you for as long as you wanted to be paid. I call this benign banishment; or

2. If they had problems with your performance or didn't like you, they would send you on undesirable assignments, like the Sahara desert in mid-summer or north of the Arctic Circle in winter. This

would make you so miserable you'd quit. Problem solved. I call this malignant banishment.

In fairness, most of our leaders were very nice and wanted to do the right thing; they knew firings cause hardship. What they failed to see about either approach was that the consequences were far more damaging than if they had simply fired the employee at the time.

Most people want to do a good job. So regardless of whether they're banished benignly or malignantly, they'll continue to try to do that. I know this because toward the end of my tenure, I was benignly banished.

I didn't realize it at first, so I just kept trying my hardest. In the end, I was working at about 30 percent of my capacity; this was debilitating to my self-esteem. Once a daily facilitator, I grew to believe I wasn't capable of facilitating at all. My enthusiasm, energy, and commitment transformed into depression, malaise, and disengagement. I ended up on medication.

Desperation finally triumphant, I resigned. With relief, the CEO confessed he'd known for months that there was nothing for me. **«**

Many leaders make the mistake of thinking that delaying difficult decisions will make it easier for employees or for themselves. While their intentions are good, the outcome is often opposite to the one they desire. In the end, employees are disengaged, demotivated, and can even develop health problems. In Gallup's ongoing surveys on employee engagement, they consistently find that disengaged employees are responsible for the majority of organizational sick days. Resilient leaders know that not making a decision can be even more damaging than making a difficult one to begin with.

Resilience for the Future

If resilience is about recovery and adjustment, then this century offers us numerous opportunities. Society is changing at a breathtaking speed. Innovation and the ability to adapt to constantly evolving realities are qualities required in everyone, but even more critically in leaders. In times where traditional heroes have fallen from pedestals, trusted institutions have failed us, and security has necessarily become an obsession, the last thing we can afford is a vacuum of role models. We need resilient leaders who can help us withstand the turbulent winds of change.

Leaders in all organizations can emerge as those role models by working with and living the 10 Laws of Leadership Resilience. There are no doubt other laws you'll learn throughout your career, but these provide a good roadmap to get started. While there will be numerous bumps along the way, in leadership, as in life, it's the journey that counts.

Shona Welsh

Shona Welsh used to be a corporate change agent but she's okay now. An award-winning speaker and writer, she works with numerous clients to provide management development and mentoring services through her company, Momentum Learning Inc. A talented keynote speaker in the area of resilience, Shona takes audiences on a journey of renewal, building on the message that courage isn't absence of fear but mastery of fear.

Shona holds a masters degree in workplace learning, is a certified coach facilitator, and a certified human resources professional (CHRP). She is the author of the acclaimed *Mentoring the Future: A Guide to Building Mentor Programs that Work* (2004), and a contributor to *Expert Women Who Speak, Speak Out! Volume 6*.

Shona and her husband have five children and are the authors of *Yours, Mine, and Hours: Relationship Skills for Blended Families* (2007). Shona cannot be left alone in the house with chocolate.

Business Name:	Momentum Learning Inc.
Address:	54 West McDougall Road, Cochrane, AB T4C 1M4
Telephone:	403-932-8882
Email:	shona.welsh@momentumlearning.com
Web Addresses:	www.momentumlearning.com
	www.yoursminehours.com
Speaking Affiliations:	Canadian Association of Professional Speakers,
	Calgary Chapter (Professional Membership)

Cara MacMillan

BMO Nesbitt Burns

Sustainable Investment

Sustainability means doing things better—not doing without.

David Suzuki

Sustainability is becoming one of those overused words that we all have to include in our vocabulary. Yet, as many elementary grade school teachers can attest, we may not be using our new word appropriately in a sentence. *Webster's Dictionary* defines sustainability as "using a resource so that the resource is not depleted or permanently damaged." Now let's define a resource. It can be defined as a natural feature that enhances the quality of human life. So, if we put the two together, sustainability is using a natural feature that enhances the quality of human life so that it is not depleted or permanently damaged. Gee, that is what my kindergarten teacher used to say: When you borrow something, make sure that you bring it back in the same or better condition. A resource can include people, animals, vegetation, minerals, water, air, the earth, as well as manufactured goods.

Webster's defines investment as a commitment for future advantage or benefit. Traditionally we have looked at investment as the placement of money for an expected gain. It includes stocks, bonds, mutual funds, or savings accounts. However, for the purpose of this chapter, we will broaden that definition to include the consumer, an individual's or corporation's time and energy, as well as the traditional financial commitment.

Sustainable investment is a commitment to a resource that enhances the quality of human life, so that it is not depleted nor permanently damaged, for future advantage or benefit.

So, when we invest we expect more. We expect to grow our money for the future. In other words, we expect to create wealth. Wealth is different from making money. Wealth lasts. Warren Buffet has long been recognized as one of the greatest investors of our time. His philosophy of purchasing solid companies that are on sale has made billions. A solid company has more than a great balance sheet. It has a great group of people who do their best every day. Their best includes performance, values, and ethics. All of these together create a solid, sustainable investment.

> *Why not invest your assets in the companies you really like? As Mae West said, "Too much of a good thing can be wonderful."*
>
> Warren Buffett

In this chapter, we'll be journeying into the new/old world of sustainable investing. We will expand the definition of investing to include any placement of a resource that allows for future benefit. This means that, as consumers, when we purchase items for our homes, our vehicles, our families, and ourselves, we are investing in our lifestyle. As employees, how we invest our time, how we create policies, and how we act in our various roles are all a choices for a sustainable world—or not. Finally, how we invest our savings can be toward improving this world for ourselves and future generations—or not.

We will be evaluating how each of us can commit our resources to enhance human life and future advantage for all. You will be challenged to make a difference: the choice is yours. We are in a period of transition in our economic model. We can choose to lead, we can choose to follow, or we can choose to put our heads in the sand. I hope that I can lead you to choose to make a difference.

> *The first rule of sustainability is to align with natural forces, or at least not try to defy them.*
>
> Paul Hawken

Awakening the Workplace

Corporate Sustainability—As a Consumer

As a consumer, every time you make a purchase, you can choose to understand the consequences of that decision. For example, when you purchase toilet paper, is the paper recycled or is it from old-growth forest? For so long, we had not even asked that question. However, if we do not think about how we financially support the companies who produce our everyday products, then how can we criticize their environmental performance? We are, in reality, financing their behavior.

Many firms understand corporate responsibility. They understand that they have a responsibility to all stakeholders to do their part in creating a sustainable world. One of my favorite stores is The Body Shop. The Body Shop was one of the first companies to sell only beauty products that were not tested on animals. As our society evolved, so did The Body Shop's leadership in social responsibility. Today they see their role as a corporate citizen that not only makes money but also has a positive influence in the world. From the website www.thebodyshop.ca, the six key tenets of The Body Shop are:

1. Against animal testing;
2. Support community trade;
3. Activate self-esteem;
4. Defend human rights;
5. Protect our planet;
6. Stop violence against women.

The Body Shop has practiced what they preach. Their activism includes a "Save the Whales" partnership with Greenpeace. They have organized many successful letter-writing campaigns with Amnesty International. They have participated in the "Light a Fire" against child poverty and "STOP Violence Against Women" campaigns. In 1996, The Body Shop created the first fully integrated *Values Report*, consisting of independently verified statements on social, environmental, and animal protection issues. The publication of the *Values Report* sparked the United Nations Environmental Program to recognize The Body Shop as a "trailblazer."

The emerging trend within The Body Shop is to ensure that all their ingredients and products are purchased from global communities who are paid a fair price and whose producers are given access to a global market that otherwise would be out of reach. For example, cocoa butter is purchased from the Kuapa Kokoo Ltd., cooperative in Ghana. The cooperative includes more than 40,000 small-scale farmers whose profits are shared within the community, which now has safe water in village wells, schools, and medical care. The Roaring Water Bay Seaweed Cooperative in Ireland naturally grows its seaweed without any chemicals or fertilizers. The plant is cut by hand to ensure that the root is intact. This is completely sustainable harvesting, as the plant is able to regrow. The cooperative offers the Irish community much-needed employment. In 2008, The Body Shop and its loyal clients ensure that more than 25,000 people in more than 20 countries worldwide earn a fair wage and work in a fair working environment.

So, every dollar you spend can make a difference. What choice are you prepared to make? Will you purchase what is immediately convenient to you? Or will you choose to invest your consumer dollars to create a better future for yourself and your world?

Corporate Sustainability—As an Employee

Sustainable development is critically dependent on the activities of business throughout the world. On the one hand, businesses are the dynamos of society, providing most of the goods and services we need, innovating to create new opportunities and possibilities, and providing most of the jobs and employment in the world. On the other hand, they have been responsible for much of the pollution and depletion of natural resources in the world, and have sometimes been bad employers and bad neighbours in the communities in which they operate. The challenge for businesses in the twenty-first century is therefore to find ways of operating as good employers and good neighbours and in ways that minimise pollution and depletion of resources.

UK Sustainable Development Commission (2004)

Recently, I was asked to speak on sustainability to a group of female executives. As I was speaking about profitability and making a difference, I noticed a woman who was becoming more and more agitated. Finally, I asked her if she had a comment. "This is just marketing. It is not real. Besides, who are you to judge?"

Now, as a speaker, I am used to people disagreeing with me, but I have to admit, this one was definitely an "ouch." I took three breaths and answered, "How you choose to react to this information is your choice. Yes, consumers are demanding sustainable options. A true marketer listens to the demands and trends within their target market."

Then to my amazement, she answered thoughtfully, "Well, actually, this could also be a way to reduce fixed and variable expenses. We could maybe influence the paradigm that the only way to reduce fixed costs is by job cuts." Then we began as a group to brainstorm on how we could look at this problem from a cost-savings perspective for the corporations:

1. **Is recycling cheaper than garbage removal?** Some companies are faced with decreased municipal services. Is there a business case to switch to a recycling company for paper, plastics, and other products? One lumber company started to recycle its wood shavings to animal shelters. The shelter pays the cost of transportation, which is less than the purchase of new shavings. It was a win-win financially for both parties.

2. **Turn the lights off! And the computers...** A quick way to improve building costs significantly is to decrease the amount of energy used. Most computers have energy-saving settings, which should be used, but machines can also be turned OFF at night, and especially over weekends and holidays. Put lights on timers so that they go off at night, and use energy-efficient bulbs. Maximize software storage for data backup to save the operational and capital cost of the servers and storage devices. Suggest working with solar or wind energy from a local utility.

3. **Paperless workplace...not quite:** We are not at the point where we have managed to create a paperless office. Yet there are ways that we can decrease the negative impact on the environment:
   - Use recycled paper as notepads;
   - Print on both sides of the page;

- Use software that eliminates blank printout pages;
- Encourage your clients to work with you online;
- Donate replaced computers and peripherals to local schools or amateur sports groups so they, too, can minimize their use of paper.

4. **Telecommute:** With today's technologies, we can be very effective working from a home office. And each day we do not travel to the office, we save carbon emissions from the commute. Our employer saves the overhead costs of office real estate.

These ideas are not new. To lead our corporations in sustainability is to present them in a business terms that will enable us to be heard and give ourselves the opportunity to make a difference in the workplace.

Like many Canadian children, our son loves hockey. Recently he was working on a school project on climate change. You can imagine his pride when his research illuminated the fact the NHLPA (National Hockey League Players Association) had joined David Suzuki's initiative to go carbon neutral. Andrew Ference, currently with the Boston Bruins, had a discussion with his teammates. They recognized that they each could make a difference *and* play hockey. So, what started as a discussion ballooned to 523 professional hockey players personally purchasing offsets to neutralize the 10 million tonnes of carbon dioxide that they each produce through travel, games, and practices. This is an example of one employee believing that teamwork extends from the ice to the planet. Andrew Ference, with his teammates and colleagues, are ensuring that young fans can enjoy their favorite game of hockey and still enjoy quality of life. These guys are true heroes (see: www.davidsuzuki.org).

The challenge for a corporation is indeed to become a sustainable business that respects all its stakeholders, including our natural world. Corporations are comprised of people. People can make an individual choice to respond to this new challenge for their corporations. Would you like to be a more valued employee? Think green. Interestingly, more and more employers are faced with the challenge of greening their businesses. Customers are demanding this commitment, as are investors. Fiscal responsibility has always been critical for the sustainable success of a business. Corporations are desperately looking for leadership in the area of sustainability. This is an opportunity for *you* to lead with your heart. Sustainability requires a new breed of leadership. It requires confident individuals who can communicate the benefit to all stakeholders. In times of change, fear is pervasive. Leaders take action and bring hope.

> *The leaders of tomorrow will have moved on from being a*
> *"good neighbour" to being "a caring and enabling partner"...*
> *They will have understood their local social and economic foot-*
> *print and will be actively engaged in local partnerships in order*
> *to reduce it. Working with a whole range of local groups and*
> *organizations, they will both encourage and enable by offering*
> *their skills, time, and passion.*
>
> Forum for the Future report
> "Corporate leadership today and tomorrow" (2003)

Corporate Sustainability—As an Investor

When we were expecting our first child, my life partner took me to meet his investment advisor. As our baby kicked happily inside me, I explained that I did not want to invest in offensive weapons or tobacco, since I hoped our child's world would be peaceful and tobacco-free. Our family had lost loved ones in war, and tobacco had killed my mother. I rattled on about other ideas until the investment advisor interrupted and asked my husband, "Do I have to work with her, or are you the decision maker?" My life partner touched my arm and smiled, "Actually you won't be working with either of us."

So began our journey into sustainable investing. The problem, as we see it, is simple—we would like to grow our investments without hurting those we love. This is not a new trend. Research shows that many religious groups have always had guidelines on investing. For example, during the 1700s, Quakers were encouraged to avoid profiting from investments that supported the slave trade. Investing in alignment with your faith is still what sustainable investing is all about. There are four key tenets to sustainability:

1. Concern and a commitment to protect the environment;
2. Understand the environmental implications of our resource usage and choices;

Cara MacMillan

3. Demand corporate accountability to the values of justice, openness, financial performance, and mutual respect; and

4. Protect human rights and human security.

There is ongoing debate as to whether or not climate change is real. However, some corporate leaders are pioneering new ways to reverse the impact of carbon dioxide on our world. One visionary who is answering this call is Sir Richard Branson of the Virgin Group of Companies.

> *What sets climate change apart from these other crises is that most people can't see the problem—CO_2 gases are invisible. If you could see them and they were colored red, 50 years ago it would have looked like a small brush fire smoldering around the world, and today it would look like a wildfire raging across the globe. We desperately need leaders who can help bring visibility and forge solutions to this imperceptible menace before it's too late.*
>
> Sir Richard Branson

Many leaders are cooperating to raise the bar on environmental stewardship. Work has been done in the past decades to create a standard by which companies can be measured. Criticism of the standards has been pervasive. There are so many different standards in the corporate circles that sometimes it is challenging to find out which ones are real and which ones are marketing propaganda. The Ceres Principles (formerly the Valdez Principles) establish standard criteria by which investors can assess the environmental performance of a firm. These companies commit voluntarily to go beyond legal requirements. From the website www.ceres.org, the Ceres Principles are:

- Protection of the biosphere;
- Sustainable use of natural resources;
- Reduction and disposal of wastes;
- Energy conservation;
- Risk reduction;

- Safe products and services;
- Environmental restoration;
- Informing the public;
- Management commitment;
- Audits and reports.

So often we criticize banks, so let's look at how they are doing with this approach. Recently a Ceres report showed that the global financial sector is evolving its leadership role in risk management to include the consideration of climate change and the cost of carbon emissions. This segment has a market capitalization of nearly $6 trillion. With its support, governance, and leadership, the global financial sector will play a vital role in supporting cost-effective solutions to reduce global greenhouse emissions. Signs of strength include:

- Nearly 100 research reports on climate change and related investment in the past 18 months;
- More than 50 percent of the global banks have an internal operations target to reduce greenhouse gas emissions;
- More than 50 percent of the global banks will continue to support alternative energy projects through direct financing or investment in renewable energy or other clean energy.

Banks are beginning to be role models in governance as well. Management policies and lending procedures are beginning to include climate change in a systemic manner. A few banks have even started to calculate the cost of carbon in the risk management process, as well as demanding a sustainability plan as part of the commercial loan process. But, of course, more could be done. Direct board involvement or linking climate change governance to CEO performance is an ideal next step. Other steps global banking could take include aggressive reduction strategies for decreasing their own carbon emissions production. But the inertia has been overcome and we look forward to where the banks can continue to lead us.

Many companies are leading us to a sustainable world. Many others are not. You have a choice with your investments. You can make money or you can make money and protect those you love. This is not a judgment; it is a fact. This is a tricky road to choose. There is a plethora of confusing and contradictory research out there. If you are sincere about sustainable investment, choose an investment advisor who specializes in this area. Be open with your advisor; discuss your values and your goals. Together, you will work on a strategy to achieve your goals, and then, together, you will build an implementation plan. Communication will be critical to success, so ensure that you are confident that you can build a solid working relationship with this individual or team.

Sustainable investment defines a philosophy of investing that is committed to creating wealth. What is very important to remember is that when you invest, you need to be authentic. Your goals for yourself, your family, and your world must be in alignment. When they are, the rewards are truly world-changing. The following is a list of the top 10 things you can do to integrate the approach into your life and your investments:

1. THINK about how you are investing your money;
2. Use the web to RESEARCH the corporate responsibility of the firms in which you invest your money and your time;
3. TALK about sustainable investment with family, friends, and neighbors;
4. ASK about your company's corporate sustainability practices;
5. EXPECT wealth;
6. COMMIT to an authentic approach to your investments as a consumer, employee, and investor;
7. DEMAND sustainable financial products from your wealth advisor;
8. RECYCLE at work, play, and home;
9. HAVE fun with it. Otherwise, life is boring; and
10. BELIEVE that one day we will all be able to use "sustainable investment" in an action sentence.

Money is a tool that enables each of us to live our values. We each need to treat our money with respect. Money must become a conscious investment in our future. Together we can choose to consume, employ, and invest our money, time, and energy for future advantage and benefit. We can choose to create sustainable wealth for ourselves by including it in the choices that we make today. We can make our kindergarten teachers proud—we can use our money to put this world back in better shape than when we borrowed it.

Cara MacMillan

Cara MacMillan is an investment advisor with BMO Nesbitt Burns, who passionately practices sustainable investment. A member of the Social Investment Organization, she is a regular contributor to community and national publications on sustainable investing. Cara teaches sustainable investment in seminars with children and adults alike; she hopes that she can inspire others to make money and to make a difference.

Cara's professional background includes executive positions in strategic management, mergers and acquisitions, customer service, and professional services. She holds a BA from Carleton University and an MBA from Athabasca University.

Cara is married to David and together they are blessed with a son and a daughter. As a parent, Cara understands the power of her actions. She consciously works to practice her beliefs and commits herself personally and professionally to sustainability. Cara involves her pre-teens in their Mom's life passion, with hope that they, too, may one day choose to live their own individual passion.

Company Name:	BMO Nesbitt Burns
Address:	1600 Carling Avenue, Suite 700, Ottawa, ON K1Z 1B4
Telephone:	613-798-4237
Email:	cara.macmillan@nbpcd.com
Web Address:	www.caramacmillan.com

Real integrity is doing the right thing, knowing that nobody's going to know whether you did it or not.

Oprah Winfrey

Ruth Sirman

CanMediate International

The High Co$t of Super Conflicts in the Workplace

If we think back to when we first graduated from high school or university, most of us entered the job market as keen, eager, and enthusiastic young adults with wonderful ideas on how we could apply what we had learned, make things better, and, in some way, change the world. And think of the reality check that we experienced as we gradually became conversant with the intricacies of the organizations and workplaces (large or small) in which we found ourselves. Organizations are somewhat like human beings. They come in all shapes and sizes with an infinite number of mandates, purposes, and objectives, and they cover the entire spectrum of possibilities in terms of how well they do what they are supposed to do. Yet, despite all the differences, there are some basic similarities that provide a common foundation for all organizations and a fascinating area for exploration.

All organizations are a compilation of people, processes, and mandates. So let's create an organization. First, let's decide what it should accomplish—its mandate. Then, let's figure out how it will manage to meet that mandate. To do this, we'll need to put in place some processes, policies, procedures, guidelines, and action plans. Now we will need some people to put the whole thing into action. Each of the people who join our organization will bring their skills, knowledge, and energy. However, in addition, they will also bring their personality, expectations, history, baggage, and possibly a few "warts" as well. Now take all of these people, the mandate, and the processes, policies, guidelines, and action plans, plus the individual and collective expectations of the people and the group and put them all into one big pot called "the workplace." Stir thoroughly and wait in breathless anticipation for it all to "work." Now in some cases it does, but in far more cases, as an entity, it will stumble along managing to maintain some level of functionality while its actual potential is sorely under-realized. What goes wrong? Why do some organizations or businesses seem to thrive and prosper, achieving significant success in terms of their mandate, profitability, and capacity to inspire loyalty from the people involved? And why do some organizations suffer from a systemic paralysis that seems to drain their lifeblood at every level—to the point that, as a system, they typically suffer a painful and inglorious end? And what about the vast majority of organizations that exist somewhere in between—managing to do some things well, but never really achieving the degree of success, profitability, and robust viability that characterizes the truly magnificent organization?

In a truly effective organization the mandate is clearly communicated to everyone at all levels, and people are actively engaged and working to get the job done and meet that mandate. They understand the link between creating a successful organization and continuing to receive their paycheck, as well as gaining the satisfaction of a job well done. In addition, roles and responsibilities are clearly defined and the resources required to achieve the goal are readily available and exist at a reasonable level. And relationships between the work teams and groups within the organization that need to work collaboratively will be well developed, supported by management and leadership, as well as the members of those different work teams and groups.

Can anyone relate to this picture? Unfortunately, for most of us the answer is "No." In reality, the majority of organizations fail to create an organizational culture that includes the level of sustainable communications required to share clearly the mandate, inspire loyalty, and build effective relationships—both at the individual and at the group level. The percentage of dysfunctional organizations and workplaces—particularly when assessed from the perspective of the employees—is significant. The co$t of this level of dysfunction is substantial—not only in terms of financial cost but also in terms of the loss of potential and the human cost.

The Co$t of the "Quick Fix"

While there are many factors that can contribute to dysfunction in an organization, the presence of conflict can elevate that dysfunction to extreme levels.

Conflicts occur in every organization on a daily basis. They can devour substantial amounts of time and resources from everyone involved as they create levels of distraction that can shut down production and foster an atmosphere of tension and angst. The impact this can have on a workplace is significant. Typically, as conflict evolves and more and more people become aware of it, the cumulative amount of time frittered away by the group rapidly increases. In turn, this can seriously undermine the ability of the group to meet production targets, leading to an overall decrease in productivity and increased costs to the organization in terms of dealing with the conflicts that may ultimately result in a loss of competitive advantage.

Managers, HR professionals, union representatives, employers, and employees strive to deal with conflicts as quickly and effectively as possible, given the time and resources they have at their disposal. However, this does not ensure that the situation will actually be resolved. Frequently, the solutions applied are superficial at best.

When conflict is not resolved or poorly resolved, it can recur—in some cases many times over, showing up in varying formats. Efforts to resolve the conflicts are typically 1) event-specific, and 2) focused on settling the issues as quickly and painlessly as possible. While in the short term this seems like a perfectly logical strategy, there is a downside. The approaches used tend to involve a superficial analysis of the situation, and the solutions are generally of the "quick-fix" type. While this can seem an effective strategy, it can also lead to long-term problems, such as the evolution of resolution resistant "super conflicts." In medical terms, think of the way that drug-resistant bacteria have evolved from the "quick fix" of antibiotics. Like the problems created for the medical profession and the patients infected by these drug-resistant bacteria, the implications for organizations can range from difficult to catastrophic in terms of the organization's viability.

The Evolution of "Super Conflicts"

So how do super conflicts evolve? Let us look at the parallels between the evolution of drug-resistant bacteria in hospitals and that of resolution-resistant super conflicts in organizations and workplaces. The processes are remarkably similar and the prognosis is equally difficult in both situations.

Figure 1: The Evolution of a Super Conflict

Stage	Super-bacteria Infection	Result	Super-conflict Infection	Result
Stage 1	Infection occurs.	Patient becomes ill.	Conflict erupts.	People get angry/hurt and work is disrupted.
Stage 2	Patient seeks help help and is treated using standard solutions, which eradicate the susceptible illness-causing organisms. The resistant organisms are left untouched by this treatment.	Patient gets better in the short term as treatment eradicates enough of the illness-causing organisms to allow the patient a temporary recovery.	Efforts are made to resolve the presenting issues using standard strategies employed by this system. Underlying systemic issues are often unrecognized or disregarded as not important or not connected.	On the surface, in the short term, things may actually appear to get better as the solutions generated during the initial resolution attempts are implemented.
Stage 3	The patient becomes ill again and the initial treatment protocol is repeated with minor changes—increased dosage, longer treatment, change in	Patient may show signs of improvement, but at each recurrence, the recovery is less successful.	Conflicts continue to erupt throughout the organization— but are often perceived to be separate and unrelated. Similar strategies are	The initial improvement is short-lived as the root causes of the problem continue to operate in the background. Each successive effort is

	medication This pattern can repeat itself many times.		employed to address each one as it arises.	less effective than the previous one as the members of the organization attempt to deal with their frustration.
Stage 4	Resistance is still replicating through the system by the reproduction of the drug-resistant organisms.	Patient gets sick again, often after appearing to be getting better. Patients and their families begin questioning medical personnel as to why they are not getting better.	The partial resolution achieved in the initial efforts creates a false sense that things are resolved, when in reality the conflict has just gone underground where the unresolved aspects continue to fester and grow.	On the surface, each intervention seems to be resolving that situation, but problems start popping up all over. Ongoing efforts to address the conflicts are perceived to be ineffective, creating a sense of "dis"-ease, tension and a level of angst within the group as perceptive people begin to question what is happening.
Stage 5	The drug-resistant bacteria reach critical mass and trigger a crisis in the patient.	Improvement and relapse cycle will continue as long as patient has energy and capacity to fight, the right treatment is found, or the patient dies.	Efforts are made to deal with each of the situations that arise separately, often using the same strategies used in the initial efforts to resolve things. The under-lying connections	Disbelief/ disillusionment about the strategies that have been used mounts. It is not the actual process itself that is at fault but rather: • faulty selection of which processes

			may still not be identified, leaving the group to deal with each separate incident/problem piecemeal.	will work best; • incomplete or flawed assessment of the issues; • lack of awareness of the root causes and the inter-connections at a systemic level.
Stage 6	Medical personnel seek additional resources/help to understand the illness and how to address it. New and more powerful approaches/solutions are required—a more targeted, comprehensive, and specific approach based on the available information about the root cause, what has worked/not worked so far and a recognition of the complexity and severity of the situation.	Patient may improve if right treatment/ combination of treatments is found and applied with sufficient intensity, duration, and resources to overcome resistance.	Residual conflict patterns and dynamics/ unaddressed issues continue to ferment and grow under the surface gaining in strength and intensity and resulting in a super conflict. Perceptive leadership will recognize the need for additional expertise and assistance to understand the root causes of the problem and find new and more comprehensive strategies to address the situation.	A thorough and complete assessment of the situation, both present and historical, is conducted by experienced and knowledgeable professionals. New strategies introduced by more experienced consultants (internal or external) are met with skepticism and fear by group. Trust and credibility in new consultants and new processes must be generated in order to move forward.

| Stage 7 | Drug-resistant infections can often lead to significant damage to host— even death— depending on extent and duration of illness. | Patient will likely need rehab and/or support to recover full functionality if that is possible. | Left unresolved, the super conflict could leave the group with a toxic work environment characterized by high turnover, low morale and productivity, and a deteriorating bottom line. | Group will typically require an intensive, comprehensive, and expensive intervention process to address issues and facilitate the transition to a healthy working lenvironment. The longer it has been unresolved the more challenging it can be to resolve. |

Organizational Breeding Grounds for Super Conflicts

What factors contribute to an organization becoming infected with conflicts that have achieved the level of super conflicts?

1. A risk-averse, rules-focused, reactive organizational culture that controls employees through rigid adherence to policies, procedures, and protocols that stifle creativity and discourage employee initiative (from the employee's perspective);

2. A leadership style and organizational culture that deals with failure through denial, finger pointing, scapegoating, blaming, and/or retribution (from the employee's perspective);

3. An organizational structure that lacks an effective and robust feedback mechanism to facilitate the multidirectional flow of information between the operational parts of the organization and the "adminisphere," which is populated by senior management and the leadership of the organization. Without this feedback loop, the leadership is cut off from the impact of their decisions, making it difficult for them to learn from any mistakes made;

4. A lack of priority on developing the soft skills of communication, conflict management, relationships, and a resultant lack of resources invested in helping members of the organization develop the requisite skills and knowledge to build the organization's capacity to resolve the problems it faces;
5. A working environment that includes:
   - High levels of stress;
   - Work/life imbalance;
   - Pressure-cooker atmosphere—tight deadlines, unremitting pressure to get things done, heavy workloads, production-focused organizational culture;
   - Lack of recognition of the impact this type of atmosphere has on employees and managers alike;
   - Lack of regular constructive recognition for the contributions of individuals and teams in getting the job done.

Normally, no one starts out with the objective of creating a massive mess in an organization, just the opposite. People characteristically do the best they can with the information, resources, and skills that they have available to them. But there are times when, despite people's best intentions and genuine efforts to try to address the conflicts and tough situations they face, the results can be less than ideal.

Managing conflict effectively is not a natural skill for most people. While there are some who seem to know intuitively how to address conflicts when they encounter them and whose resolution success is significant, there are those at the other end of the scale who seem to create and catalyze conflicts wherever they go. But the majority of people fall somewhere in the middle—stumbling along doing the best they can but typically lacking the resources required, in terms of understanding, knowledge, and skills, to be able to resolve conflicts effectively and quickly before the issues escalate into major problems.

It's only in the past few years that the unacceptably high cost of poorly resolved conflicts has been recognized as an organizational issue. As the level of awareness of the impact that conflicts can have on the overall success of organizations grows, leading-edge organizations that have a strong commitment to creating and maintaining a healthy workplace atmosphere now rank conflict management skills among the core competencies used to select and promote people, particularly at the management and leadership levels.

In addition, super conflicts rarely arise as the result of a major crisis that can easily be identified and pinpointed as the source of the problem. Rather, super conflicts tend to be much more insidious in their evolution—gradually brewing and growing in strength—often in the background and in seemingly unrelated areas. This creates a challenge in terms of early identification of a super conflict. To do this, it requires a bird's-eye view of the organization and the knowledge of what to look for. Having this more objective view can be very difficult to achieve from within the organization. However, a super conflict will eventually make its existence known when some incident happens and, like a volcanic eruption, catalyzes the entire state of affairs to erupt and become visible. At this point, the organization is likely to degenerate into crisis as things seem to be falling apart everywhere, people are stunned at what's happening, and it becomes so overwhelming that it's hard to know where to start to try to fix it.

Is Your Organization Infected?

So, how do you tell if your organization is laden with super conflicts? The following are some of the key warning signs:

- Elevated employee turnover rates, particularly among newer employees who may have started the job, realized that something was wrong, and chosen to leave rather than get caught up in it—or the reality they experience is not what they were told they could expect;
- Escalating demands on the EAP program and its service providers;
- Increasing numbers of employees on burnout or stress leave;
- Disengaged and disenfranchised employees in the organization often showing up as a pattern of grumbling and complaining, or "shut down" among employees that is pervasive and ongoing;
- Externally motivated employees who seem to be marking time between paychecks and who demonstrate no active engagement or interest in the life of the organization, other than what it can do for them as individuals;

- A lack of trust or a pervasive negativity among the various groups in the organization—employees, managers, leadership, union(s), human resources;
- Ongoing employee identification of issues and concerns and requests for assistance that are ignored by management, or are acknowledged but go unaddressed. These can often be related to workload, poor relationships with other groups within the organization, or inadequate communication;
- Perceptions (articulated or not) that management/leadership does not care about employees.

In addition to the warning signs above, there are other indicators of the possible presence of a super conflict in your organization, including:

- A pattern of dealing with conflict within the organization by the most expedient methods available that will get things back to "normal" and people back to work, at least on the surface, even if it is merely settled and not resolved. The challenge here is that the strategies chosen to deal with the problem are generally based on minimizing the time and resources allocated (both human and financial) rather than on getting to the root of the problem. And, if people are not given the opportunity, the support, and the resources required to actually explore the deeper issues and develop comprehensive strategies to resolve them, the solutions that are implemented are typically superficial at best. This is like putting a Band-Aid over an infection in the hopes that, since we can no longer see the sore, it will heal and go away. The reality is that, while often done with the best of intentions, this approach tends to drives the conflict underground where it continues to fester and grow into an abscess;
- A history of multiple conflicts within the organization that are perceived by employees to have been unresolved, only partially resolved, or poorly resolved. In many cases, this goes hand in hand with the problems outlined above. This would typically include multiple ongoing incidents that may have involved different people but have the common denominator that, from the perspective of those involved and those "watching the situation," they have not truly been resolved. People don't feel that they have achieved any level of closure and there is still a level of discontent/unhappiness with whatever decisions were made by whoever "settled" the problem. Interestingly enough, management

typically believes that the situation has been addressed and is unaware of employees' frustration and inability to move forward. In many cases, this is typified by an organization's traditional approach that is less than constructive in its approach to conflict and its focus on minimizing the problems and getting them out of the way as quickly as possible;

- The presence of employees who at some level still carry a residual level of bitterness, frustration, anger, hurt, or cynicism as a result of both of the above-noted situations. When situations are well resolved, those involved in the situation are able to walk away ready to move forward and with a sense that the resolutions reached have been fair, practical, and will actually make a difference. Poorly resolved conflict leaves a bitter taste in the mouths of those affected.

Time, Timing, and Super Conflicts

"Time" and "timing" are also factors that need to be taken into consideration when exploring the impact, consequences, and outcomes of conflict within an organization. As stated earlier, often the deep-rooted problems within an organization that contribute to the evolution of a super conflict are difficult to detect in the early stages. This can lead members and leaders of organizations to miss subtle but critical clues that all is not well until the problems reach a crisis state where they can no longer be ignored. The problem is that by the time this level of visibility is reached, the organization is often on the brink of crisis. This evolution typically follows an exponential growth curve—it starts slowly and, as the momentum builds, it picks up speed until it reaches that critical mass where the momentum is so great that it explodes. Figure 2 shows what it would look like if the super conflict evolved over a 30-day period.

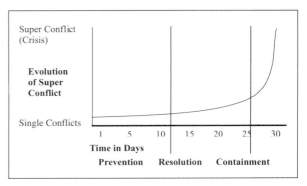

Figure 2: The Evolution of a Super Conflict

What does this mean for organizations in conflict? In order for an intervention to be successful at managing conflict, it is critical that the strategy used is appropriate to the situation. It is important to know where the organization is at on the evolutionary time curve so that this choice can be made effectively. Figure 3 shows which strategies fit most effectively with different parts of the evolutionary time curve.

Figure 3: Time-Curve-Appropriate Management Strategies

Days #	What you see	What is needed	Type of strategy	Example
1–12	Very subtle, difficult to discern conflict dynamics.	High levels of awareness and perception; willingness to look forward and plan.	**Prevention:** Investment in building capacity to provide skills, knowledge required.	Training, including conflict management and harassment awareness, development of conflict management policies, promotion of healthy working relationships and communication.
13–25	Separate conflicts occurring, often triggered by current events but fed by systemic, deep-rooted issues.	System view of organization, ability to see this bigger picture, process and analyze dynamics.	**Resolution:** Access to resources that can help group use these strategies constructively.	Mediation, negotiation, group interventions, coaching.
26–30	Crisis mode— upset, angry people, serious conflicts escalating in intensity and frequency.	A willingness to acknowledge the severity of the situation, the ability to de-escalate it, or the willingness to seek help.	**Containment/ Damage Control**	Guidelines for behavior, peace-keeping strategies, listening and acknowledgement of severity of situation, ready access to resources that can help.

In regard to conflict, the issue of an organization's location on the time curve has significant implications for what is required to resolve situations of conflict. The ultimate objective, no matter where an organization is located currently on the time curve, is to find ways to move back down the curve to the lowest position possible—and then employ strategies that will effectively maintain that position. With this 30-day model, let's look at how time and timing determines the required action:

- **Between days 1–12:** It is very difficult to recognize the dynamics of what is happening, as there are few overt signs of the potential dysfunction. At this stage, the conflicts are reasonably isolated, even if they are major in scope. Their presence does not necessarily mean long-term problems *if* they are completely resolved to the satisfaction of *all* concerned, and the group achieves closure and is able to move on. At this stage, forward-thinking managers and leaders will be actively planning and providing sound prevention strategies for their organization. This entails investing in building relationships, promoting a healthy workplace atmosphere, and modeling the type of communication and behavior that will prevent problems from arising down the road.

- **Between days 13–25:** The organization finds itself in a state where the signs of systemic dysfunction are somewhat more obvious but can still be missed (or ignored). At this stage, an organization needs solid resolution strategies and recourse mechanisms in place to effectively manage the problems that arise. This can include mediation, negotiation, group conferencing, coaching, and so on. In addition, ongoing training and access to employee assistance programs, union representatives, human resources, and staff relations support persons can provide those involved in tough situations with a level of front-line assistance that can help to resolve things early on.

  The critical factor here, however, is leadership. Whether it is formal or informal, leadership is less important than the message being given and the willingness to listen and hear the important information required to achieve the level of awareness and knowledge necessary to be able to address the growing issues. Often, the most important messages are those that are *not* being articulated—particularly, what is being avoided, what are the "non-discussables" and where are the fears and concerns. When leadership is able to draw this information out and act on it constructively to address the concerns, they can help to move their organization back down the curve to the lower levels where the focus can shift to prevention mode.

- **Between days 26–30:** The situation rapidly escalates to crisis level. For many organizations where the more subtle clues were missed or ignored, this crisis level may take people by surprise—with both its arrival and its intensity. Often people will say, "I don't know what happened! Everything was fine until yesterday and now it seems everything is falling apart! How could this happen?" When the situation reaches this level, the situation needs to be contained to prevent further escalation. This is damage control at work in an effort to bring the situation back down the time curve to where the situation can be resolved.

It is critical in assessing the situation to understand where it is on the time curve and to choose strategies that fit the current reality. It makes no sense to bring in prevention strategies when an organization is in crisis; containment is what is needed.

So, ultimately, the ideal is to employ strategies that will help an organization get to and maintain a position on the time curve somewhere between days 1–15 over the long term. But it is not enough just to get to that stage; the critical factor here is the willingness to recognize that conflict itself is not bad and that its positive potential is lost when it is ignored. After all, nothing ever changes without conflict in some form. It is the willingness to assess your organization objectively and with brutal honesty and then to invest in resolutions that have the capacity to address issues thoroughly that can immunize an organization against super conflicts. Ultimately, an organization that is willing to invest in achieving this goal and is able to maintain that position will be in good shape to weather the storms of conflict when they hit and will have the flexibility and robustness to survive in the world of business or government.

Ruth Sirman

Ruth Sirman is a speaker and trainer of unshakeable substance. She will keep you on the edge of your seat, leading you forward to new solutions and endless possibilities. Her creative genius shines as a developer of programs that have impacted thousands of lives in areas of conflict resolution, restorative justice, mediation, and leadership. Ruth's knowledge of human behavior, her quick wit and humor-based "down home" practicality have made her a sought-after speaker, trainer, mediator, and writer.

Drawing from her own life experiences, Ruth has successfully facilitated seminars for many branches of federal, provincial and municipal governments, Queen's University, the United Church of Canada, the Government of Nunavut and various business associations, positively impacting thousands of participants.

Ruth's company, CanMediate International, promotes a more palatable approach to life by using the techniques and strategies Ruth has developed to guide people through the processes to resolve tough complex conflicts, manage difficult relationships, create sustainable change in their lives and live to tell about it.

Business Name:	CanMediate International
Address:	272 Gore Street, Almonte, ON K0A 1A0
Telephone:	613-256-3852
E-mail:	rsirman@canmediate.com
Web Address:	www.canmediate.com
Professional Affiliations:	Canadian Association of Professional Speakers; Conflict Resolution Network Canada; ADR Canada; ADR Ontario; Workplace Mediation Association; Society for Conflict Resolution of Ontario

Mama exhorted her children at every opportunity to "jump at de sun." We might not land on the sun, but at least we would get off the ground.

Zora Neale Hurston

Because a Missed Idea
Is a Missed Opportunity

Each week, when sending out my email newsletter, a ton of automated "out of office" responses come back. With the exception of a few details—name, date of return, person to contact in the case of emergency—they are all exactly the same. Compare this to an auto-responder that my friend Susan created last summer when she was going to be out of the office for a couple of weeks.

> **»** If you are receiving this message, it is because I am being held hostage by two children under the age of six. They have locked me out of my office and hidden both my cell phone and my Blackberry. They are monitoring my brainwaves to ensure that I do not try to even think about work. I can see the message light flashing on my phone and I can only imagine the number of emails invading my inbox as we speak, but I am helpless and unable to respond. Do not be alarmed. My captors are treating me well and have advised me that if I provide them with my undivided attention for the next two weeks, I will be allowed to return to my office on August 4. If you have not heard from me by then, please advise the local authorities. **«**

Upon receiving Susan's email, I couldn't help but smile. Reading it over again, I chuckled to myself each time. Susan had turned an ordinary auto-responder into an unexpectedly extraordinary experience. Several months ago, I had another unexpected extraordinary experience:

» I had decided to go out for dinner to a neighborhood Italian eatery that I frequent from time to time. The restaurant is ordinary but the food is good and reasonably priced, and on this particular evening I was in the mood for pasta that I didn't have to prepare myself.

It was a quiet evening so I had the dashing young waiter, Stephane, pretty much to myself. I placed my order and in what seemed like no time at all, a plate of pasta appeared before me. Stephane then returned with a huge wooden bowl of one of my true weaknesses in life—freshly grated parmesan cheese. As he raised a large spoon overflowing with the fluffy white flakes of my Achilles heel, he leaned over and asked in a voice infused with a smoky French accent, "Would you prefer cheese like snow in Denver or cheese like snow in Paris?" In an instant, a completely predictable evening was transformed into an unexpectedly extraordinary experience that I will always remember. «

What do these stories have in common? Both Susan and Stephane had taken a completely ordinary moment and had transformed it into an unexpectedly extraordinary experience. A simple auto-responder had become a vivid story, complete with mischievous children and a willing co-conspirator. A simple request about cheese had become a journey to faraway places. In the process, both Susan and Stephane had taken me out of the intellectual sameness of the totally predictable and grabbed my attention with the emotional excitement of the unexpected. Both Susan and Stephane had understood that *a missed idea is a missed opportunity*.

Perhaps you are a business owner anxious to improve the positioning of your product or service in the marketplace. Perhaps you are a manager with an essential message to communicate to your employees or to your colleagues. Perhaps you work in the not-for-profit sector and need to create awareness and inspire action around membership or fundraising.

Whatever the job or challenge in your workplace, the reality remains the same. In today's information overload, shrinking-attention-span world, messages can't get heard if they don't get noticed first.

Awakening the Workplace

In my role as a professional innovation catalyst, I work with organizations of all kinds helping them to cultivate a culture of innovation in the workplace. This culture is called *the Innovation Advantage—more ideas from more people more often.*

Your organization's Innovation Advantage is completely dependent upon its ability to cultivate, from each and every member of the team, ideas that ensure that key messages get noticed so that they can then get heard. Innovation Advantage is about your ability to turn ordinary moments into unexpectedly extraordinary experiences that your customers, employees, colleagues, and members will never forget. Innovation Advantage is about your ability to create a workplace where both individuals and teams are free to imagine the possibilities!

Innovation Advantage equals more people with more ideas more often because a missed idea is a missed opportunity.

Getting Noticed

In a crowded marketplace, fitting in is failing. In a busy marketplace, not standing out is the same as being invisible.

Seth Godin, *The Purple Cow*

Getting noticed is all about creating "unexpected encounters." Think, "cheese like snow in Denver or cheese like snow in Paris?" Think, "I am being held hostage by two children under the age of six." These are examples of unexpected encounters.

Imagine the power of creating "unexpected encounters" with your product, service, or message. What could you do to take your message to your target market in a way in which they would least expect it? Be Bold. Be Innovative. Be Unexpected.

Imagine the possibilities! The following are some examples to get you started. How could you create an unexpected encounter with:

An important message that you need to communicate to a colleague?

_____

_____

_____

An important message that you need to communicate to a potential customer?

_____

_____

_____

An important message that you need to communicate to your boss?

_____

_____

_____

The Four S's of Innovative Unexpected Encounters

Creating unexpected encounters that get our message noticed is one thing, but getting noticed just for the sake of getting noticed is not enough. For an unexpected encounter to be truly innovative, it needs to meet the S's of Innovative Unexpected Encounters.

Surprise: Is it unexpected? Will it get noticed?

Strategy: What's in it for us? Will it accomplish our predetermined objectives?

Seduction: What's in it for them? Will the target audience perceive value?

Sustainability: Can we sustain it? Do we have the resources?

The following is a great example of an unexpected encounter that meets all four S's:

>> It is an unusually hot and sunny early fall day as you stroll down a bustling street in a pseudo trendy area of town. With a good 15 minutes to go before the start of your lunch meeting, you decide to explore the selection of eclectic wares adorning the street for the neighborhood sidewalk sale.

Straight ahead, you notice a rather unique-looking woman, vivid in both style and personality. As you pass in front of her rather ordinary display, she calls out, "Your choice. Your price." You stop. You back up. You notice that, in fact, there is not a single price tag in sight. She repeats, "Your choice. Your price. All of the profits go toward helping suicide prevention in your community." The eccentric sales lady engages you in conversation, introduces herself as "Monika with a k," and proceeds to tell you about her life as a volunteer.

You're hooked. Not only are you hooked, you're curious, and before long, you are spending money that you never intended to spend on something that you never intended to buy.

That's because "Your choice. Your price. All of the profits go toward helping suicide prevention in your community," is a perfect example of the four S's that transform unexpected encounters into innovative business strategies. **«**

Does "Your choice. Your price," meet the four S's of innovative unexpected encounters?

1. **Surprise: Did it get noticed?** On a street crowded with products and price tags, Monika with a k was the exception to the rule. The product was not surprising but the sales approach was. It got your attention. It got you to stop and listen.

2. **Strategy: Did it accomplish predetermined objectives?** Monika with a k's predetermined objective was to sell more product. She figured out that most people would end up spending more money if there were no price tags than they would if there were price tags. This unexpected encounter got the job done.

3. **Seduction: What's in it for them?** Surprise without a promise of value is short-lived. Monika with a k understood that her product itself was not exceptional. However, nothing is more satisfying—both intellectually and emotionally—than the promise of a great deal. And if *that* promise didn't work, the emotional tug of contributing to a good cause for *your* own community was waiting in the wings.

4. **Sustainability**: **Can we sustain it?** Monika's strategy perfectly matched the resources that she had at her disposal.

All four S's need to be present for an idea to be transformed into an Innovative Unexpected Encounter. For example, if you have an idea for an unexpected encounter that won't get noticed, your message won't get heard. If you have an idea that is surprising but doesn't accomplish your objectives, you are being different for the sake of being different and that's irrelevant. If your idea is surprising and strategic, but the target listener sees no value in your message, you will be easily forgotten. And finally, a great idea that requires resources that you don't have is doomed to remain just an idea. (Unless, of course, you can *imagine the possibilities and create an innovative resourcing strategy*!)

Developing Your Innovation Advantage

The following is a template of steps you can use to help incorporate the Four S's of Innovation into your workplace or business challenge:

What message do you want to get noticed? _____
_____
_____

Who is your target market or audience? _____
_____
_____

What is your idea for creating an unexpected encounter between your message and your target audience?
_____
_____

How can you ensure that your idea meets the four S's of Innovative Unexpected Encounters?

Surprise: _____
_____
_____

Strategy: _____
_____
_____

Seduction: _____
_____
_____

Sustainability: _____
_____
_____

Enabling Innovation in Yourself and Others

People here don't start with conclusions. They start with questions.

Tim Armstrong, President of Advertising
and Commerce in North America, Google

To ignite innovation in yourself and others, putting systems and a culture in place that supports it is key. This allows more people to have more ideas more often. Here is an example from one of the most successful companies in the world:

» The magazine headline jumped out at me: "15 Reasons Google Is No. 1." I couldn't believe it. This was it—a list. I love lists. People can follow lists. I can follow lists. Lists make things easy. I mean, lists list things— steps, ingredients, reasons—and all you need to do is follow the list to get the desired result. So I'm thinking to myself, this is HUGE. All I need to do is follow this list of 15 reasons why Google is the most innovative company in the world and I can be innovative too.

I grabbed the magazine. Expectantly I rushed to page 53 and suddenly, there they were. People; 15 people to be exact. Fifteen of the most amazingly audacious, courageously creative, and inspirationally innovative people you would ever want to meet, and they all work for Google. In fact, as I read through the article, it became clear that any of Google's people could have been one of these 15 people because Google hires people who think differently. People who ask different questions. People who find different answers. **«**

Google people have more ideas, more often. The corporate culture ignites innovation in others right from the hiring process. They seek out people who ask different questions and people who find different answers. How are people hired in your organization? Are they hired for their capacity to *do* or for their capacity to *think*? Are they hired for their ability to *answer* questions or for their ability to *ask* them?

Once we have the right people, there are three essential steps to increasing the volume of ideas in any workplace:

1. Encourage unexpected questions;
2. Apply imagination to information; and
3. Cultivate constant courage.

#1—Encourage Unexpected Questions

» Recently I was in Nova Scotia to speak at a phenomenal event that brings together business people from throughout Atlantic Canada. The evening before my presentation, I was in my room getting ready for dinner when there was a knock at my door. I opened it and a hotel attendant handed me a plate with two individual-sized tubs of ice cream. "Is everyone from the conference getting ice cream?" I asked. "No, Miss Newman," the young man replied, "it's just for you."

I was special. I was appreciated. I was impressed! "How did they know that I love ice cream?" I wondered as the exquisite rum and raisin flavors melted in my mouth. "Must be a coincidence," I concluded.

At dinner, I heard about another speaker who had found his favorite dessert in his room the evening before. In fact, the recipe for this dessert had been hunted down and supplied to the chef at the hotel for this one special occasion. This was no coincidence.

As I thought back over my unexpected encounter with my favorite dessert, I remembered that when I had been hired for the event, the meeting planner, Colleen, had sent me a questionnaire that included the question, "What is your favorite dessert?" The penny dropped. The mystery was solved. «

Organizations that master Innovation Advantage encourage people to ask unexpected questions because they know that the answers to those unexpected questions hold the key to creating opportunities for unexpected encounters. How could your organization do more to encourage the members of your team to ask unexpected questions?

#2—Apply Imagination to Information

Encouraging people to ask unexpected questions is an integral step to anchoring innovation in your organization's culture. However, the key to creating Innovative Unexpected Encounters lies in what we do with the answers to those questions. The key lies in our ability to apply our imagination to that information. Not only did Colleen, the meeting planner, ask an unexpected question, she used her imagination to design an unexpected encounter with the information. She used the information to inspire an idea.

Have you ever wondered where ideas come from? Where do you get your best ideas? Personally, I get my best ideas in the shower. In fact, if I really think about it, my best ideas come any time I'm near water. Showers, baths, sitting by the ocean or boating on a lake—they all work for me.

What about you? Where do you get your best ideas? I ask this question of most of my audiences and here are the most popular answers:

- In the shower (and I thought I was so unique!);
- Driving in the car;
- Exercising;
- Just before falling asleep, during the night, or when waking up;
- On vacation or during leisure time.

You might notice that no one says that they get their best ideas at work. What could be the reason for this? Could it be that our workplaces have become more about *doing* and less about *thinking*? Could it be that our workplaces place more value on *information* than *imagination*? Could it be that we have simply lost the habit of engaging in imaginative thought at work?

Research has shown, time and time again, that the real potential to make unique and innovative connections lies in our subconscious mind. This subconscious mind is freed up when we are in the shower, driving in our car, or doing exercise. During these times, our brains are distracted and that creates space for our imaginations to come out and play—time for us to apply our imaginations to the information that is anxiously waiting to be transformed into an idea.

The following are some personal and workplace techniques that will kick-start your and your co-workers' imaginations. You'll be set free to have *more ideas more often at work.*

Out of My Mind—Back in 15 Minutes.

>> Each morning before starting my workday, I take 15 minutes to sit and think. It's not planning, solving, or doing time. It's simply thinking time. With me is a journal where I have written inspirational quotes, and as I read these inspiring thoughts, I allow my mind to wander. There is even a sign on my door to let people know that I am not to be interrupted. It reads, "Out of my mind—back in 15 minutes." «

My 15-minute ritual is dedicated to creating space in my brain, to creating a small reservoir of imagination that I can apply to the information that I will receive during the day. It sets the tone that will permit me to have *more ideas more often*!

As important as it is for individuals to create space in their brains, if we truly want to anchor the Innovation Advantage in our culture, we need to create space in our collective brains as well. The strategies that follow will create opportunities for teams to apply imagination to information:

Leave Air in Your Agendas

Most of you would probably agree that we spend an awful lot of time in meetings. Daily meetings, weekly meetings, on-site, off-site—the list is endless. In fact, many of those meetings come with agendas that seem endless too. However, another way to get to *more ideas more often* in the workplace is to plan for a little less information and little more imagination by leaving more air in your meeting agendas. Here is how you do it:

For longer meetings (1 day or more) consider the following format: one or two speakers followed by scheduled roundtable discussions of the information that has been presented. The focus of the discussion is not only to share key "take aways" from the presentation but also to begin a process of collective reflection based on an informal exchange of ideas, insights, and inspirations. Make sure to leave yourself enough time for these discussions. On average, I suggest leaving 30 to 45 minutes of air after each block of two hours of presentations. You also might want to consider having a facilitator at each table—usually someone from your organization—that can direct the discussion, take notes, and ensure that everyone has the opportunity to contribute.

For shorter internal meetings try leaving 10 minutes of air at the beginning of each meeting dedicated to stimulating imaginations and preparing participants' brains for the task of imagining the possibilities! In fact, you might want to try a little group brain exercise.

Drop and give me 20. No, not push-ups—ideas. Here's how it works: Divide participants into groups and give one object—any object—to each group. Advise the groups that they have four minutes to imagine 20 things that the object could be *except* for what it really is.

After about a minute, interrupt the flow of conversation and ask them to continue the exercise; however, now they need to imagine that they are all only five years old. What would the object be if they were five years old? After another minute, add another trigger. If the participants were aliens from another planet, what would the object be? Then finally, in the last minute of the exercise, if they were blind, what would the object be?

Chances are that everyone will have come up with at least 20 ideas. If you ask for feedback from the group, some will most likely tell you that the game was fun because anything was possible. Others might tell you that they found the exercise difficult because they are not used to coming up with ideas under pressure (in other words, they've lost the habit). Overall, though, you can be assured that most of the group will have forgotten about deadlines, conflicts, and to-do lists—at least for now. You will have left some air in your agenda, created some space in their brains, and they will be ready to *imagine the possibilities*!

For the very brave, you might even want to consider occasionally not having a meeting agenda at all. Concerned about not getting anything accomplished?

Consider this: Canon CEO Fujio Mitarai holds a one-hour meeting every morning with no formal agenda and *this* is the meeting that executives refuse to miss.

#3—Cultivate Constant Courage

> *First they ignore you, then they ridicule you, then they*
> *fight you, then you win.*
>
> Mahatma Gandhi

Know that you may find some inner or workplace resistance to shifting to incorporating the Innovation Advantage in your life. Ideas for innovative unexpected encounters are great in theory, but it often takes great courage to turn those ideas into results. Keep in mind, that:

Without courage, there are no ideas;

Without courage, there is no discussion of ideas;

Without courage, there is no change.

When it all comes down to it, creating Innovation Advantage in any organization is an exercise in constant courage.

Have the courage to SEE your ideas—the courage to wade through the murky waters of comfort and resistance to the place of clarity where you have the courage to see things that you have never seen before.

Have the courage to BELIEVE in your ideas—the courage to believe that your ideas have the power to make a difference and that *you* have the power to make them happen.

But because no idea can meet its full potential alone, have the courage to SHARE your ideas—the courage to share in spite of your fear of ridicule, risk, and remorse; the courage to put yourself on the line because if you don't, you know that you and all that you care about will be left standing still.

Finally, have the courage to ACT on your ideas—the courage to act because there really is no such thing as failure. There is only an opportunity for growth, learning, and moving forward. After all, the only real risk is the risk of being left behind.

You now know how to have more people having more ideas more often. Follow the Four S's of Surprise, Strategy, Seduction, and Sustainability to create Innovative

Unexpected Encounters. Encourage unexpected questions, create opportunities for both individuals and teams to apply imagination to information, and cultivate constant courage to anchor the Innovative Advantage in the culture of your organization. Stay the course and stick with the process because *you* know that **a missed idea is a missed opportunity**—a missed opportunity to...

Make a difference;

Do what you do better;

Have more of an impact;

Get your message heard;

Leave a lasting impression;

Get someone's attention;

Stir things up;

Rock the boat;

Cross the finish line first;

Say "Why not";

Say "What if";

Awaken your workplace;

Imagine the Possibilities!

Toni Newman

Professional catalyst **Toni Newman** is a five-time award-winning business owner with an uncanny ability to help her clients turn information into innovation and ideas into results.

In today's challenging marketplace, where competitive advantage is determined by our ability to effectively differentiate ourselves from the competition, highly respected leaders from sectors as diverse as finance, retail, telecommunications, health care, and insurance count on Toni's 25-plus years of real-world business knowledge and uniquely creative insight to provoke the kind of thinking that results in innovative strategies specifically designed to propel their organizations forward.

In addition to being a busy keynote speaker and idea facilitator, Toni has been a contributing author to the successful series *Women Who Speak, Speak Out* and is listed in the National Register's *Who's Who in Executives and Professionals*. She is past president of the Montreal chapter of the Canadian Association of Professional Speakers, as well as a past board member of the Montreal chapter of Meeting Professionals International and the Montreal Marketing Association.

Toni's company, *The Innovation Advantage,* is based in Montreal where Toni lives with her two children. As a family, they are dedicated to learning through fun and to exploring the power of the imagination.

Business Name: The Innovation Advantage
Address: 1 Ramses II, Kirkland, QC H9J 3V6
Telephone: 514-697-9855
Email: toni@toninewman.com
Web Address: www.toninewman.com
Speaking Affiliations: Canadian Association of Professional Speakers (Past President, Montreal Chapter)

Favorite Quotation:
Things are only impossible until they're not.
                Jean-Luc Picard, *Star Trek: The Next Generation*

Kathy Glover Scott, M.S.W.

Kathy Glover Scott is the mastery guru. As a keynote speaker and facilitator, she weaves together best business practices with advanced energy work to help attain powerful results. As an executive and business coach, Kahty teaches mastery and how to live optimally each day. In addition to being the co-publisher of this internationally best-selling book series, Kathy is the author of the acclaimed *Esteem!*, and *The Successful Woman* (also published in Europe and Asia). She is in demand as a cutting-edge keynote speaker and leader in innovative energy practices.

Kathy is one of only four people in North America accepted to teach Reiki to the 21st degree, as well as other advanced energy-based courses. Visit her website for speaking topics, online courses and upcoming programs in your area.

Kathy is currently working on two writing projects focusing on mastery and shifting consciousness.

Books and CDs by Kathy Glover Scott:

- The Successful Woman
- Esteem! A Powerful Guide to Living the Life You Deserve!
- The Craft of Writing for Speakers (CD)

Experts Who Speak Books (co-publisher):

- Expert Women Who Speak...Speak Out! Volumes 1–6
- Sales Gurus Speak Out
- Leadership Gurus Speak Out
- Awakening the Workplace, Volumes 1, 2 and 3

Business Name:	Kathy Glover Scott & Associates
Address:	P.O. Box 72073, Kanata North RPO
	Kanata, ON K2K 2P4
Telephone:	613-271-8636
E-mail:	Kathy@kathygloverscott.com
Web Address:	www.kathygloverscott.com
Professional Affiliations:	International Federation of Professional Speakers, Canadian Association of Professional Speakers (Ottawa Chapter)

Adele Alfano

Canada's Diamond Coach **Adele Alfano** is renowned as an expert in personal effectiveness and excellence, and change management. She has earned the reputation of being a "mining" expert in professional potential and personal empowerment. Nominated for Canada's 100 Most Powerful Women, Adele has been acclaimed for her energetic and content-rich keynotes and informative seminars. She has been described as a skillful and entertaining presenter who combines charm, wit, heart and passion.

As an award-winning professional and inspirational speaker since 1998, Adele has been a sought-after opening and closing conference keynoter, luncheon speaker, employee/volunteer recognition awards speaker, and seminar leader. Renowned for her proven techniques, she is privileged to have an extensive client list that includes large national associations, leading corporations, government, school boards, and the health care industry. Adele consistently receives rave reviews and standing ovations from audience members who find her presentations valuable, touching and informative.

Canada's Diamond Coach is the co-author, co-editor/ publisher of the *first ever* series of collaborative books by experts and speakers, entitled Experts Who Speak Books— www.expertswhospeakbooks.com.

Business Name:	Diamond Within Resources: Speaking and Consulting
Address:	P.O. Box 60511, Mountain Plaza Postal Outlet
	Hamilton ON L9C 7N7
Telephone:	905-578-6687
E-mail:	adele@diamondwithin.com
Web Address:	www.diamondwithin.com
	www.kissmytiara.ca
Professional Affiliations:	International Federation of Professional Speakers, Professional
	Member of the Canadian Association of Professional Speakers

Notes

Notes